5/4/16

Social Issues
in Literature

Slavery in Toni Morrison's *Beloved*

Other Books in the Social Issues in Literature Series:

Class Conflict in Emily Brontë's *Wuthering Heights*

Colonialism in Joseph Conrad's *Heart of Darkness*

Depression in Sylvia Plath's *The Bell Jar*

The Environment in Rachel Carson's *Silent Spring*

Genocide in Ann Frank's *The Diary of a Young Girl*

Poverty in John Steinbeck's *The Pearl*

Race in Ralph Ellison's *Invisible Man*

Race in William Shakespeare's *Othello*

Teen Issues in S.E. Hinton's *The Outsiders*

War in Kurt Vonnegut's *Slaughterhouse-Five*

Women's Issues in Kate Chopin's *The Awakening*

Women's Issues in Margaret Atwood's *The Handmaid's Tale*

Women's Issues in Zora Neale Hurston's *Their Eyes Were Watching God*

Women's Search for Independence in Charlotte Brontë's *Jane Eyre*

Social Issues
in Literature

Slavery in Toni
Morrison's *Beloved*

Dedria Bryfonski, Book Editor

GREENHAVEN PRESS
A part of Gale, Cengage Learning

GALE
CENGAGE Learning·

Detroit • New York • San Francisco • New Haven, Conn • Waterville, Maine • London

GALE
CENGAGE Learning·

Elizabeth Des Chenes, *Director, Publishing Solutions*

© 2012 Greenhaven Press, a part of Gale, Cengage Learning

Gale and Greenhaven Press are registered trademarks used herein under license.

For more information, contact:
Greenhaven Press
27500 Drake Rd.
Farmington Hills, MI 48331-3535
Or you can visit our Internet site at gale.cengage.com

For product information and technology assistance, contact us at

Gale Customer Support, 1-800-877-4253
For permission to use material from this text or product, submit all requests online at
www.cengage.com/permissions

Further permissions questions can be emailed to permissionrequest@cengage.com

Articles in Greenhaven Press anthologies are often edited for length to meet page require- ments. In addition, original titles of these works are changed to clearly present the main thesis and to explicitly indicate the author's opinion. Every effort is made to ensure that Greenhaven Press accurately reflects the original intent of the authors. Every effort has been made to trace the owners of copyrighted material.

Cover image © jeremy sutton-hibbert/Alamy.

LIBRARY OF CONGRESS CATALOGING-IN-PUBLICATION DATA

Slavery in Toni Morrison's Beloved / Dedria Bryfonski, book editor.
    p. cm. -- (Social issues in literature)
Includes bibliographical references and index.
ISBN 978-0-7377-6389-8 (hardcover) -- ISBN 978-0-7377-6390-4 (pbk.)
1. Morrison, Toni. Beloved. 2. Slavery in literature. I. Bryfonski, Dedria.
PS3563.O8749B4356 2012
813'.54--dc23
                                                                        2012002510

Printed in the United States of America
2 3 4 5 6   17 16 15 14 13

Contents

Introduction   9

Chronology   13

Chapter 1: Background on Toni Morrison

1. The Life of Toni Morrison   18
   Denise Heinze and Catherine E. Lewis

   Toni Morrison weaves together fact and fiction, folklore
   and history, the real and the supernatural, to translate
   the African American experience into the broader context of what it means to be American.

2. Morrison Creates a Black History That Is an   32
   Essential Part of the American Dream
   Sture Allen

   With generosity of spirit, Toni Morrison creates from
   myth and history the fabric of the black experience in
   America.

3. Morrison Based *Beloved* on a True Story   36
   Cincinnati Enquirer

   A news story appearing in a nineteenth-century Ohio
   newspaper details the real-life murder of a black infant
   that Toni Morrison used as the basis for her novel *Beloved*.

Chapter 2: Slavery in *Beloved*

1. *Beloved* Shows How the Power of Love Helped   42
   Black People Survive Slavery
   Carolyn C. Denard

   Many students assume that Toni Morrison's intention in
   Beloved is to show the horrors of slavery. That is only
   part of the story—her real intent is to show how black
   men and women managed to maintain their humanity despite being enslaved.

2. Morrison Uses Slave Songs to Show   54
   the Humanity of Slaves
   Peter J. Capuano

Slave songs are an important part of the African American oral tradition. While it was dangerous to speak of the horrors of slavery, slaves were able to confront and come to terms with their demeaning experiences through song.

3. Racial Solidarity Is the Only Solution to Slavery and Racism   67
Doreatha Drummond Mbalia

African Americans continue to confront racist attitudes as oppressive as those that existed during slavery. Just as the characters in *Beloved* survive slavery by their love and support for each other, African American people today can conquer racism by coming together.

4. The Character Beloved Depicts the Loss of Cultural Identity That Occurred During Slavery   76
Lisa Williams

The character Beloved represents not only Sethe's murdered infant but all the Africans who endured passage to America on slave ships. Depicted as a ghost, she symbolizes the displacement of Africans who were separated from their history and culture.

5. An African American Identity Was Forged by Slavery   84
Timothy L. Parrish

African Americans forged an identity as a people through their shared experience of slavery. Slaves created supportive communities to preserve their humanity. These communities helped them to develop resilience and to reclaim their history and culture.

6. Slavery Robbed African Americans of Their Personal Identities   91
Jennifer L. Holden

The schism between Sethe and Beloved—with neither one understanding their true connection as daughter and mother—represents the personal dislocation created by slavery, as Africans were separated from their land, culture, religion, and families. Slavery reduced African Americans to objects and denied them their essential natures as unique individuals.

7. *Beloved* Exposes the Psychological Trauma   **103**
Caused by Slavery
J. Brooks Bouson

Slaves were subject to both physical abuse and psychological humiliation, resulting in trauma. Psychological trauma led to feelings of shame and self-loathing. Sethe murders her infant to spare her from being subjected to this degradation.

8. Morrison Examines the Divisive Impact   **117**
of Racial Oppression
Babacar M'Baye

In *Beloved*, Morrison explores the harm created by racist attitudes. The notion that whites are superior to blacks was at the root of slavery and continues to this day to impede successful relationships between blacks and whites.

9. Slavery Damaged the Mother-Child Relationship   **125**
Wilfred D. Samuels and Clenora Hudson-Weems

Slavery created irreparable damage to the mother-child relationship. It is the natural instinct for mothers to love and protect their children; however, slaves had no possessions—even their children were the property of their masters—and therefore mothers had no way to protect their children.

Chapter 3: Contemporary Perspectives on Slavery

1. Slavery Remains a Significant Global Problem   **137**
E. Benjamin Skinner, as told to Terrence McNally

Despite the fact that slavery has been officially banned worldwide by the United Nations, there are 27 million people in slavery today, forced to work under threat of violence for subsistence pay. In contrast to slaves in nineteenth-century America, who were considered valuable property, today's slaves come cheap and are considered disposable.

2. US Companies Are Complicit   **146**
   in Modern-Day Slavery
   Sarah C. Pierce

   Although human trafficking has been a crime in the
   United States since October 2000, it is a crime that frequently goes unprosecuted. Corporations are particularly
   successful at evading prosecution, as they use subcontractors to distance themselves from the victims forced
   into labor.

3. It Is Possible to Eradicate Modern Slavery   **156**
   Kevin Bales

   Most people are unaware that many basic commodities
   are created using people forced into slavery. Steel, food,
   cotton, gold, computers, clothing, and sporting goods are
   just some of the items that have been produced by victims of human trafficking. Fortunately, modern slavery is
   a problem that can be solved.

4. Human Sex Trafficking Is Big Business   **166**
   Rodney Hill and Amanda Walker-Rodriguez

   Human sex trafficking is the fastest-growing criminal activity worldwide. The problem is both global and local.
   Many victims from developing nations are forced into
   slavery and sold into the United States, and an increasing
   number of runaway teens are recruited into the sex trade.

For Further Discussion   **173**

For Further Reading   **175**

Bibliography   **177**

Index   **181**

Introduction

With her first four novels, Toni Morrison steadily built her reputation as a gifted novelist addressing serious issues in lyrical prose. The publication of *Beloved* in 1987, however, brought her reputation to an entirely new level. In this novel, Morrison returns to the familiar themes of her earlier works—the saving power of family and community, the quest for self, and how human decency can prevail under even the basest of conditions—but addresses them in a richly complex narrative with hauntingly poetic language. *Beloved* won the Pulitzer Prize for Fiction in 1988, and in 1993 Morrison was awarded the Nobel Prize in Literature, based largely on *Beloved*. According to Trudier Harris in the 1991 book *Fiction and Folklore: The Novels of Toni Morrison*,

> Throughout her novels, but especially in *Beloved*, Morrison is concerned with the individual's place in the larger community, and with questions of good and evil, right and wrong, that transcend traditional morality. All of these concerns have as one of their bases the African-American folk tradition, especially that reflected in tales of slavery and other tales passed on during slavery.

Captured from their homes in Africa and transported in unspeakable conditions on slave ships to an unfamiliar country, African American slaves were separated from their families, culture, language, and history. Deprived of any education that could enable them to learn to read or write, slaves turned to the oral tradition of storytelling to express their identity and preserve their culture. The oral tradition served another purpose—some of the stories told were too painful to commit to written form. Even after the end of slavery, storytelling retained an important and empowering role in African American culture.

The African American oral tradition, especially the telling of ghost stories, was an essential part of Morrison's family life. Both of her parents were storytellers. During her youth, her family gathered around while the parents told stories. The children were expected to participate, weaving stories of their own. Morrison's grandmother introduced her to the African American mysticism and magic that would later permeate her fiction. Morrison has frequently affirmed the important roles of storytelling and the supernatural on her life and work. In an interview with Mel Watkins for the *New York Times Book Review* in September 1977, Morrison stated, "Black people believe in magic. Once a woman asked me, 'Do you believe in ghosts?' I said, 'Yes. Do you believe in germs?' It's part of our heritage." In a 1981 interview with Charles Ruas, reprinted in *Conversations with American Writers*, Morrison elaborated on the central role that ghost stories played in her youth:

> As a child I was brought up on ghost stories—part of the entertainment was storytelling. Also, I grew up with people who believed it. When they would tell you stories about visions, they didn't tell them as though they were visions. My father said, "Oh, there's a ring around the moon, that means war." . . . My grandmother would ask me about my dreams and, depending on the content of them, she would go to the dream book, which would translate dreams into a three-digit number. That was the number you played in the numbers game. . . . My dream life is still so real to me that I can hardly distinguish it from the other, although I know what that is. It's just as interesting to me and an inexhaustible source of information. I was very conscious of trying to capture in writing about what black life meant to me, not just what black people do but the way in which we look at it.

Reinforcing the importance of the supernatural in her work, Morrison wrote in "Rootedness: The Ancestor as Foundation" in 1984:

I try to blend the acceptance of the supernatural and a profound rootedness in the real world at the same time with neither taking precedence over the other. It is indicative of the cosmology, the way in which Black people look at the world. We are a very practical people, very down-to-earth, even shrewd people. But within that practicality we also accepted what I suppose could be called superstition and magic, which is another way of knowing things. . . . That kind of knowledge has a very strong place in my work.

In *Beloved*, Morrison creates a work that is part historical narrative, part supernatural ghost story. The novel is based on a real event—fugitive slave Margaret Garner's slaughter of her infant daughter to prevent her child from being captured back into slavery, a fate Garner considered far worse than death. As the novel begins, Sethe, the character inspired by Margaret Garner, and her daughter Denver live in a house haunted by the spirit of the infant Sethe had killed many years earlier, a child known only as Beloved. The ghost of Beloved is driven from the house by an exorcism, only to return in the flesh-and-blood form of a young woman. The residents of the house soon conclude that the girl is Beloved risen from the dead to continue to haunt them; however, Beloved has memories of life on a slave ship that cannot be reconciled with the early experiences of Sethe's murdered daughter. Thus, it soon becomes clear that Beloved represents not only the murdered infant but also the souls of all Africans who suffered through the Middle Passage. And to Morrison, according to Carl D. Malmgrem in his 1995 essay "Mixed Genres and the Logic of Slavery in Toni Morrison's *Beloved*,"

The reincarnation of Beloved compels Sethe to confront her personal past, a past that up till then had been "unspeakable," to come to terms with the fact that she murdered her baby daughter. In this novel, then, "nothing ever dies," especially our private ghosts, the skeletons we think safely locked in our closets, at least until we put them to rest. Because 'anything dead coming back to life hurts,' what Sethe must undergo is an agonizing private exorcism of her own.

In *Beloved*, Morrison masterfully employs African American narrative traditions to weave her vision of the impact of slavery on the present and future, as well as on the interior lives of the people who experienced slavery. In the essays that follow, critics discuss the theme of slavery in *Beloved*. In addition, the final chapter of the book contains articles that discuss the persistent impact of slavery in modern times.

Chronology

1931

Toni Morrison is born Chloe Ardelia Wofford on February 18 in Lorain, Ohio, to George and Ramah Willis Wofford, the second of four children.

1949

Wofford graduates from Lorain High School and enrolls at Howard University.

1953

Wofford graduates from Howard University with a BA in English and a minor in Classics. She enrolls in the graduate program in English Literature at Cornell University.

1955

Wofford receives her MA in English from Cornell University. She is hired by Texas Southern University to teach English and the Humanities.

1957

Wofford joins the faculty of Howard University as an English instructor.

1958

Wofford marries Harold Morrison, a Jamaican architect.

1961

A son, Harold Ford Morrison, is born to Harold and Toni Morrison.

1962

Morrison joins a writers group at Howard University and writes a short story that will later become the basis of *The Bluest Eye*.

1964

Morrison travels to Europe and divorces on her return. Her second son, Slade Kevin Morrison, is born in Ohio.

1965

Morrison is hired as a textbook editor for L.W. Singer, a division of Random House located in Syracuse, New York.

1968

Morrison moves to New York City and becomes a senior editor for Random House, where she will publish the work of many African American writers.

1970

The Bluest Eye is published by Holt, Rinehart, and Winston.

1971–1972

Morrison teaches part-time at the State University of New York at Purchase.

1973

Sula is published by Knopf.

1976–1978

Morrison teaches part time at Yale University.

1977

Song of Solomon is published by Knopf.

1978

Song of Solomon wins the National Book Critics Circle Award and is the main selection of the Book-of-the-Month Club.

1980

Morrison is appointed by President Jimmy Carter to the National Council on the Arts.

1981

Tar Baby is published by Knopf. Morrison is elected to the American Academy and Institute of Arts and Letters, the Writer's Guild, and the Author's League. She teaches part-time at Bard College.

1983

Morrison leaves her position at Random House to devote herself to writing and teaching full-time.

1984

Morrison accepts the Albert Schweitzer Professorship of the Humanities at the State University of New York at Albany.

1987

Beloved is published by Knopf.

1988

Beloved wins the Pulitzer Prize for Fiction, the Robert Kennedy Book Award, the Melcher Book Award, and the Elmer Holmes Bobst Award for Fiction.

1989

Morrison accepts the Robert F. Goheen Chair in the Council of the Humanities at Princeton University.

1992

Jazz is published by Knopf. *Playing in the Dark: Essays on Whiteness and the Literary Imagination* is published by Harvard University Press.

1993

Morrison is awarded the Nobel Prize in Literature.

1996
Morrison is named Jefferson Lecturer in the Humanities by the National Endowment for the Humanities and is awarded the National Book Foundation Medal for Distinguished Contribution to American Letters. *The Dancing Mind*, Morrison's National Book Foundation Lecture, is published by Knopf.

1998
Paradise is published by Knopf.

1999
The Big Box, a children's book Morrison coauthored with her son Slade, is published by Hyperion.

2002
Morrison and Slade coauthor *The Book of Mean People*, which is published by Hyperion.

2003
Love is published by Knopf.

2006
Morrison retires from Princeton University.

2008
Mercy is published by Knopf.

2010
Slade dies at age forty-five.

2011
Morrison receives an honorary doctor of letters degree from Rutgers University.

Background on
Toni Morrison

The Life of Toni Morrison

Denise Heinze and Catherine E. Lewis

Denise Heinze is an assistant professor in the English Department at North Carolina State University. Catherine E. Lewis is an instructor in the English Department at Louisiana State University.

Toni Morrison was profoundly influenced by her parents, who preached to their children the importance to African Americans of family, community, and individual identity, Heinze and Lewis maintain in the following viewpoint. The role of family and the larger community as nurturing factors figures as a theme in most of Morrison's fiction, the authors argue. Morrison perceives the values of the black community to be more sustaining than those of the white community, assert Heinze and Lewis.

Morrison was born Chloe Ardelia Wofford in Lorain, Ohio, the second of four children raised in a family that had endured economic and social adversity. Morrison's maternal grandparents, Ardelia and John Solomon Willis, were sharecroppers in Greenville, Alabama, having lost their land at the turn of the century. In 1912 her grandparents decided to head north to escape the hopeless debt of sharecropping and the fear of racism, which posed the threat of sexual violation to their pubescent daughters. They traveled to Kentucky, where Morrison's grandfather worked in a coal mine and her grandmother was a laundress. But they left abruptly when their daughters came home from school one day, having taught the white teacher how to do long division. In search of a better education for their children, Morrison's grandparents eventually settled in Lorain.

Denise Heinze and Catherine E. Lewis, *Dictionary of Literary Biography—American Novelists Since World War II: Third Series*. Belmont, CA: Gale Research, 1994. www.Cengage.com. © 1994 Global Rights & Permissions, a part of Cengage Learning. Reproduced by permission.

Morrison's Family Experienced Racism

While growing up during the Depression, Morrison witnessed the struggles of her father, George Wofford, who had migrated from Georgia, and mother, Ramah Willis Wofford, to support their family. George Wofford often worked many jobs at a time—a shipyard welder, car washer, steelmill welder, and construction worker—while Ramah Wofford, Morrison revealed in a 1983 interview with Nellie McKay, "took 'humiliating jobs' in order to send Morrison money regularly while she was in college and graduate school." Her parents' willingness to take on hard and sometimes demeaning work was coupled with a distinct unwillingness to relinquish their own sense of value and humanity. Morrison's father was meticulous in his work, writing his name in the side of the ship whenever he welded a perfect seam. Her mother at one point wrote a letter of protest to President Franklin D. Roosevelt when her family received unfit government-sponsored flour.

While Morrison's parents grappled with economic hardship, they also struggled to retain their sense of worth in an oppressive white world. Their early experiences with racism shaped their respective views of white people. Morrison's father was, in her words, a racist; she told [interviewer] Jean Strouse that, as a child in Georgia, he received "shocking impressions of adult white people." Morrison's mother held out hope for the white race to improve, but her father was convinced that whites were never to be trusted or believed. He once threw a white man out of his home, believing the visitor planned to molest his daughters. Both parents had reservations about the potential for the white race and thus taught their children to rely on themselves and the black community rather than the vagaries of a larger society whose worth to them was highly suspect.

Morrison did not suffer the effects of racism early on because she was the only black in her first-grade class and the only one who could read. However, she told [interviewer] Bonnie Angelo that her innocence was soon shattered:

> I remember in the fifth grade a smart little boy who had just arrived and didn't speak any English. He sat next to me. I read well, and I taught him to read just by doing it. I remember the moment he found out that I was black—a nigger. It took him six months; he was told. And that's the moment when he belonged, that was his entrance. Every immigrant knew he would not come as the very bottom. He had to come above at least one group—and that was us.

Morrison confronted other incidents of racism, but her parents' emphasis on the value of African-Americans as a people, of their family as an inviolable unit, and of themselves as individuals was no doubt the psychological foundation that sustained and nurtured her. Her father was convinced that blacks were superior to whites, a belief that deeply influenced Morrison. At age thirteen, when she complained about the mean white family whose house she cleaned, her father told her she did not live with them, but "here. So you go do your work, get your money and come on home." Morrison did not adopt her father's racism, but she always knew, she remarked in an interview with [PBS television talk show host] Charlie Rose. "I had the moral high ground all my life."

Music and Reading Were Important

Though deprived of monetary resources in a hostile world, Morrison's family and community held a remarkable wealth of music, storytelling, the supernatural, and black language— major influences on Morrison and her writings. Morrison woke up to the sound of her mother's voice, singing both at home and for the church choir. But music, Morrison said in the Rose interview, "was not entertainment for us" but more a means of detecting her mother's moods. It acted as a support system. Though her family could not read music, they could reproduce the music they heard. Other forms of support included storytelling that involved every member of the family. After adults told stories, they invited the children to do the same. Morrison considered this part as important, if not more important, than listening to the stories.

Though there were few books in her house, Morrison learned early the importance of reading. Her grandfather was a figure of awe and respect to her because, with the help of his sister, he had taught himself to read. Morrison was encouraged to read and did so voraciously, including a wide range of world literature. . . .

A Sense of Family and Community

After high school Morrison attended Howard University, majoring in English and minoring in the classics; her dream was to be a teacher. While at Howard she acquired the nickname Toni. She soon became disenchanted with Howard and the importance students placed on marriage, fashion, socializing, and chic. She joined the Howard University Players, thus getting an opportunity to travel in the South, to experience its history and geography, and to relive her grandparents' harrowing flight from poverty and racism. Morrison graduated from Howard in 1953 and then enrolled in graduate school at Cornell University.

Morrison's rich history of family and community filters directly into her novels, a progression of works that begins by addressing the black family and then broadens to the black community, regions of the United States, foreign lands and alien cultures, history, and reality. In her novels Morrison celebrates the rich heritage and language of the black community and the values it struggles to maintain in a predominantly white society whose own value system, she finds, has lost its collective way. Morrison's thematic consistency is refigured in each novel so that her canon constitutes a progressive troping of her own works. Each novel is an original and refreshing revoicing of her previous concerns with the black community and family. She experiments almost relentlessly with language, with narrative forms, and with fictive reality in an endeavor to redefine the African-American experience not as marginal or peripheral, but as American.

Morrison received her master's degree from Cornell in 1955. She wrote her thesis on the theme of suicide in the works of Virginia Woolf and William Faulkner. She then taught English at Texas Southern University in Houston for two years, beginning a teaching career that she proudly continues to this day. According to [literary scholar Valerie] Smith, Morrison has taught at "Yale, Bard, the State University of New York at Purchase, and the State University of New York at Albany. Since 1988 she has held the Robert F. Goheen Professorship of the Humanities at Princeton University." [Morrison retired from Princeton University in 2006.]

In 1957 Morrison, then an English instructor at Howard, began to meet and influence young men who became prominent in the 1960s, among them, [writer] Amiri Baraka, [politician] Andrew Young, and [writer] Claude Brown. She taught [student activist] Stokely Carmichael in one of her classes; she told Strouse that he was "'the kind of student you always want in a class—smart, perceptive, funny and a bit of a rogue.'" Morrison stayed at Howard from 1957 to 1964, leaving because she did not have the Ph.D. necessary for tenure.

Two major events marked her period of teaching at Howard. She began to write, and she married Harold Morrison, a Jamaican architect. During her marriage Morrison joined a writer's group at Howard, composing a story that grew into her first novel, *The Bluest Eye* (1970), about a little girl who longs for blue eyes. With her writing career only in its infancy, her marriage ended around 1964, leaving Morrison with two sons, Harold Ford and Slade Kevin. Though reticent about her marriage and reluctant even to discuss its actual date, she does refer to cultural differences and a feeling of personal bankruptcy: "It was as though I had nothing left but my imagination. I had no will, no judgment, no perspective, no power, no authority, no self—just this brutal sense of irony, melancholy and a trembling respect for words."

After her divorce Morrison lived with her parents in Lorain for a year and a half and then accepted an editorial position with a textbook subsidiary at Random House in Syracuse, New York. Her mother expressed dismay that Morrison was a single parent without other family there—a difficult, isolated condition for anyone, but especially for African-Americans, who to a great extent rely on extended family and community for well-being in an indifferent, if not inhospitable, world. Morrison talked to Rose about raising children alone: "It was terrible. Very hard. Awful." She added, "You need everybody [to raise a child]." For Morrison writing helped fill the void of family, husband, and, to a great extent, self. She remarked to [novelist Gloria Naylor in an interview]: "But I was really in a corner. And whatever was being threatened by the circumstances in which I found myself, alone with two children in a town where I didn't know anybody, I knew that I would not deliver to my children a parent that was of no use to them. So I was thrown back on, luckily, the only thing I could depend on, my own resources."

Success as a Writer and Editor

While in Syracuse, Morrison continued work on *The Bluest Eye* as a way to find her place in a world where she felt she no longer belonged. She told Naylor that writing the novel became a process of reclamation:

> And I began to do it. I began to pick up scraps of things that I had seen or felt, or didn't see or didn't feel, but imagined. And speculated about and wondered about. And I fell in love with myself. I reclaimed myself and the world . . . I named it. I described it. I listed it. I identified it. I recreated it. And having done that, at least, then the books belonged in the world.

Toni Morrison poses beside a reproduction of the cover of Time *magazine that featured her on January 19, 1998.* © Robert Maass/Corbis.

An editor read the partly completed manuscript and suggested she finish it. It was rejected many times before Holt, Rinehart and Winston published *The Bluest Eye* in 1970.

The Bluest Eye is a wrenching account of how the Western notion of idealized beauty and its penchant for blue eyes and blond hair turn self-esteem in the black community into self-loathing. The novel reveals the destructive potential of a standard of beauty that places value on the way people look rather than on their intrinsic worth. . . .

In the late 1960s and early 1970s Morrison's career as a writer paralleled her increasing prominence in the publishing world and as one of the cultural elite of the black community. She left Syracuse to become a senior editor at Random House in New York City. There, she established herself as a mentor for such aspiring African-American women writers as Toni Cade Bambara, Gayl Jones, and Angela Davis. Bambara told Strouse that Morrison is "a superb editor" whose judgment she trusts "absolutely." In the same article Young remarked that "Toni had done more to encourage and publish other black writers than anyone I know." Morrison also supported the publication of important works on black history, including *The Black Book* (1974), which she edited. Morrison was called on increasingly in the early 1970s to review books, especially for the *New York Times Book Review*, for which she critiqued twenty-eight books from 1971 to 1972. In 1971 she also wrote an article, "What the Black Woman Thinks About Women's Lib," for the *New York Times Magazine*.

The idea for Morrison's second novel, *Sula* (1973), came months after she finished *The Bluest Eye*. . . .

In *Sula* as in *The Bluest Eye*, Morrison continues her denunciation of white values and their negative impact on the black community. . . .

With the publication of *Sula* Morrison's importance as a writer was established. The novel received more critical and popular attention than *The Bluest Eye* and was excerpted in *Redbook*, selected as an alternate for the Book-of-the-Month Club, and nominated for the 1975 National Book Award in fiction. . . .

Morrison's third novel, *Song of Solomon* (1977), expands beyond the time and place of her first two books, moving from North to South and from present to past in an endeavor to uncover and rediscover the personal history of an African-

American family. *Song of Solomon* is, in some ways, a fictionalized venture of another project in which Morrison was involved, *The Black Book*, a scrapbook of African-American history published soon after *Sula*. In *Song of Solomon* Morrison for the first time uses a male protagonist, Milkman, to undergo a rite of passage—not from innocence to experience but from one history to another, one culture to another, and one value system to another. He undergoes a ritual immersion into the South and his own history in an attempt to understand himself and his culture.

As in *The Bluest Eye* and *Sula*, the black community in *Song of Solomon* struggles with a double consciousness that can wreak havoc on their lives. Not willing to give up the distinctive quality of their African-American culture, they are nevertheless pressured or lured into a desire for assimilation that in this novel takes the shape of land ownership, a crucial aspect of African-American history because it constitutes physical and legal evidence of a history and tradition. . . .

Song of Solomon was both a popular and critical success, establishing Morrison as one of America's most important novelists. The novel became a paperback best-seller, with 570,000 copies in print in 1979. *Song of Solomon* was a Book-of-the-Month Club main selection, the first novel by an African-American so chosen since Richard Wright's *Native Son* (1940). Morrison's success and recognition led to her 1980 appointment by President Jimmy Carter to the National Council on the Arts. In 1981 she was elected to the American Academy and Institute of Arts and Letters. . . .

In *Tar Baby* (1981) Morrison no longer focuses exclusively on the black family and community, setting her novel in the Caribbean and thus incorporating several different cultures, including the island natives, Philadelphia Negroes, and Western imperialists, all of whom are mutually dependent on one another but who are alienated from any sense of community.

With this hodgepodge of people comes a conflicting set of values that struggle for an impossible hegemony in a riot of interdependence. . . .

Beloved

In *Beloved* (1987) Morrison embraces the supernatural as perhaps the ideal vehicle for the investigation of slavery, an institution so incomprehensible that Morrison suggests that most Americans would like to bury it, since it is the historical reminder of a national disgrace. Morrison delayed the writing of this novel because she anticipated the pain of recovery and confrontation. She told Elizabeth Kastor, "I had forgotten that when I started the book, I was very frightened. . . . It was an unwillingness and a terror of going into an area for which you have no preparation. It's a commitment of three or four years to living inside—because you do try to enter that life." In spite of "this terrible reluctance about dwelling on that era," Morrison informed Angelo that she went ahead with the writing of the book because "I was trying to make it a personal experience."

Beloved is based on the true story of the slave Margaret Garner, who murdered her own child rather than return her to slavery. In the novel the slave woman, Sethe, escapes to freedom in the North, where she lives with her remaining children. Morrison altered the true story, she told Marsha Darling in a 1988 interview, as Garner was not tried for murder. . . .

Morrison informed Darling that she did not do much research on Garner because "I wanted to invent her life, which is a way of saying I wanted to be accessible to anything the characters had to say about it. Recording her life as lived would not interest me, and would not make me available to anything that might be pertinent." The metaphor for Morrison's reluctance for mimesis is the configuration of Beloved—part ghost, zombie, devil, and memory. Morrison reveals Beloved in tantalizing degrees until she is manifested as a full-blooded person. Like a childhood trauma Beloved comes back in snatches until finally her history is retold, a discovery process shared by Morrison, her characters, and the readers as the primary step to collective spiritual recovery.

Beloved is a purging of the guilt of the American psyche, and it acts as a historical precedent to and psychological referent for the rage of the oppressed in Morrison's other books. Sethe's slave status involves total loss of freedom and humanity and serves as the origin of all subsequent forms of oppression endured by Morrison's other characters and the motivation for their violent reactions to them. In *The Bluest Eye* Cholly's response to racial oppression is the rape of his own daughter. In *Sula* oppression caused by war turns Eva's Plum into a drug addict, forcing her to euthanatize him. Sexual oppression in *Tar Baby* drives Margaret to burn little holes in her baby. All these acts testify profoundly to the legacy of an institution so evil that it affords a mother no alternative for her children but death. . . .

Beloved earned the Pulitzer Prize, an award that had been denied another great writer, James Baldwin. In an effort to prevent the glaring oversight that Baldwin suffered and to secure Morrison's place in literary history, many African-American writers had published a tribute to Morrison in the *New York Times Book Review*, "Black Writers in Praise of Toni Morrison," that states in part: "We find your life work ever building to a monument of vision and discovery and trust." . . .

Later Novels

Jazz (1992), Morrison's sixth novel, is based on a photograph in James Van DerZee's *Harlem Book of the Dead* (1978) that shows, according to [reviewer John] Leonard in the *Nation*, "the body of a young girl, shot at a party by a jealous boyfriend, who died refusing to identify her assailant." Morrison told Rose that she wished to investigate "the question" of male/female passion, hence the story of Joe, a middle-aged cosmetic salesman; his childless wife Violet; and the teenage Dorcas, with whom Joe has an affair and whom he shoots when he is jilted for a younger lover. While *Jazz* may have begun with the issue of male/female passion, it ends as a fictive re-creation of two parallel narratives set during major historical events in African-American history—Reconstruction and the Jazz Age.

In *Jazz* Morrison continues her investigation of the debilitating impact of history on black families. In this novel she does not focus on slavery, but on its legacy to a generation removed in time but not place from its grasp. The unrelenting, destructive influence of racism and oppression on the black family is manifested in *Jazz* by the almost-total absence of the black family. . . .

In her seventh novel, *Paradise* (1998), Morrison provides for her readers a narrative that both acknowledges and redesigns techniques she has used before, while she continues to demand from language that it reach rigorously beyond its own limits. . . .

In *Paradise* Morrison continues the thematic explorations she began in the earlier works—family, love, rejection, the supernatural, geography, and journeys—and she reexamines the questions of history, place, and community that drive *Beloved* and *Jazz*. . . .

Love of Family and Community

Morrison's experimentation with the novel coincides with her ever-increasing thematic concerns. As if constricted by the necessary closure of a novel, Morrison expands the consciousness of each successive novel without leaving behind the burning issues that mark her previous ones. Thus family, community, and the love they provide or deny are a constant in her canon. History, geography, and eventually myth, fable, and the supernatural are gradually implemented to illuminate the nature of those families and communities. Morrison's first two novels, *The Bluest Eye* and *Sula*, are spatially and chronologically limited, though *Sula* introduces World War I as a historical backdrop.

Song of Solomon moves in time and place from present to past and from North to South, while *Tar Baby* is set outside the continental United States on an island where past and present frequently intermingle. *Beloved* is a historical novel that concerns Reconstruction, yet it implies ahistoricity in the amazing figure of Beloved. *Jazz* integrates historical eras and moves to the city, all the while disavowing its own efficacy to reproduce either time or place. *Paradise* relies on history and tradition to give background to the collective ideology of the men but moves away from the South/North, white/black dichotomies of the former novels to examine a closed community that must come to terms with itself.

But time and place only partially reflect Morrison's desire for circumference—[poet] Emily Dickinson's term for the endeavor to comprehend totality. Morrison always begins with a different question and then finds the characters to manifest it. The questions and the characters change dramatically in each novel. In *The Bluest Eye* sexual abuse and idealized beauty afflict a little black girl, while in *Sula* Morrison chooses two adult black women to illustrate the nature of sexual freedom and moral responsibility. In *Song of Solomon* a black male undergoes the recovery of personal history, and in *Tar Baby* another black male is a source of spiritual renewal. In *Beloved* a ghost symbolizes the horror of slavery, and in *Jazz* an even-less-visible presence admits failure in understanding the nature of male/female passion. *Paradise* examines the evolution of people who ultimately turn on others who are like themselves. But such a summary is reductive and does little to convey the myriad other themes and characters Morrison invokes. She uses children and adults, men and women, blacks and whites, haints [ghosts], and a metaphysical metafiction to give voice to the shimmering essence of humanity.

Ultimately in *Jazz* Morrison questions her ability to answer the very issues she raises, extending the responsibility of her own novel writing to her readers. Morrison's narrator at the end of *Jazz* invokes his/her readership to "Make me. Remake me." Morrison thereby sends an invitation to her readers to become a part of that struggle to comprehend totality that will continue to spur her genius.

Morrison Creates a Black History That Is an Essential Part of the American Dream

Sture Allen

Sture Allen is the former permanent secretary of the Swedish Academy.

Toni Morrison sees African American culture as an essential part of the American dream, asserts Allen in his speech presenting the 1992 Nobel Prize in Literature to Morrison. Morrison believes that blackness and whiteness are two opposing but complementary and necessary aspects of American culture, Allen suggests. With its rich, musical, narrative style, Morrison's fiction is at its core deeply compassionate and humanistic.

The Nobel Prize awarded by the Swedish Academy is, as we know, a literary prize. This year it has been granted to Toni Morrison, making her the ninetieth Nobel Laureate in Literature.

Returning History to Blacks

In her volume of essays, *Playing in the Dark*, Miss Morrison lucidly pictures the insights that she has gained, as an author and a reader in her native country: "It is as if I had been looking at a fishbowl—the glide and flick of the golden scales, the green tip, the bolt of white careening back from the gills; the castles at the bottom, surrounded by pebbles and tiny, intricate fronds of green; the barely disturbed water, the flecks of waste and food, the tranquil bubbles travelling to the surface—and suddenly I saw the bowl, the structure that trans-

Sture Allen, "Nobel Lecture for Literature Prize 1993: Toni Morrison," in *Nobel Lectures, Literature 1991–1995.* Hackensack, NJ: World Scientific Publishing Co., 1997. Copyright © 1993 Nobel Foundation. Reproduced by permission.

parently (and invisibly) permits the ordered life it contains to exist in the larger world." In other words, she regards the African presence in her country as a vital but unarticulated prerequisite for the fulfilment of the American dream. Similarly, she sees whiteness in literature as having blackness as its constant companion, the racial other as its shadow.

In her depictions of the world of the black people, in life as in legend, Toni Morrison has given the Afro-American people their history back, piece by piece. In this perspective, her work is uncommonly consonant. At the same time, it is richly variegated. The reader derives vast pleasure from her superb narrative technique, shifting from novel to novel and marked by original development, although it is related to [William] Faulkner and to the Latin American tradition. Toni Morrison's novels invite the reader to partake at many levels, and at varying degrees of complexity. Still, the most enduring impression they leave is of empathy, compassion with one's fellow human beings.

Milkman Dead, the protagonist of *Song of Solomon*, reflects one of the basic themes of Miss Morrison's novels, in his quest for self. Milkman's paternal grandfather was a liberated slave. When he was registering his freedom, he responded to a question about his father with the word "Dead", thus acquiring his macabre surname from the drunken official who asked. His family was prepared to accept this name: "It was new and would wipe out the past. Wipe it all out." The Solomon whose name occurs in the title of the novel, Milkman's peculiar southern forefather, was to be found even in the song that went with children's games. The intensity of his inner life had carried him through the air back to the Africa of his origins. Solomon's rapture was ultimately Milkman's as well.

Motifs in space and time continue to be interwoven in *Beloved*. Paradoxically, the combination of realism and folklore enhances the novel's credibility. In the world which the female protagonist, Sethe, inhabits, one does not possess one's own

Toni Morrison discusses her play Dreaming Emmett *during an interview in Albany, New York, on December 23, 1985.* © Bettmann/Corbis.

body. There is tremendous power in Toni Morrison's description of Sethe's act of releasing her child, Beloved, from the destiny she imagines her facing, and of the consequences of this act for her own life, in which Beloved's double personifies the burden of Sethe's guilt.

In her latest novel, *Jazz*, Toni Morrison's approach is similar to the style in which jazz is performed. The opening lines of the novel state its theme, the lives of a number of people in Harlem in the 1920s. In the course of the novel we perceive a first-person narrator, varying, supplementing and intensifying the story. The final picture is a highly composite image of events, characters and atmospheres, mediated in sensual language with a deep inherent sense of musicality. Toni Morrison's way of addressing her reader has a compelling lustre, in a poetic direction.

Humor and Humanity Respond to Cruelty

When she was very young, her family's landlord set fire to the house in which they lived when her parents fell behind with the rent. And while they were in it. Her family reacted to this absurd form of crudeness, monumental crudeness, not with resignation but with laughter. This, says Toni Morrison, is how you can distance yourself from the act and take your life back. You take your integrity back.

In great minds, gravity and humour are close neighbours. This is reflected in everything Toni Morrison has written, and evidenced in her own summary: "My project rises from delight, not disappointment."

Dear Miss Morrison,

I have just told the audience that, in your own words, your project rises from delight, not disappointment. As you disclose fundamental aspects of hidden reality, you make gravity and humour abide side by side in your remarkable work, with its verbal music. It is my privilege and pleasure, on behalf of the Swedish Academy, to convey to you our warmest congratulations on the Nobel Prize in Literature for 1998, and to invite you to receive the Prize from the hands of His Majesty the King.

Morrison Based *Beloved* on a True Story

Cincinnati Enquirer

First published in 1841, the Cincinnati Enquirer *is a daily newspaper serving the greater Cincinnati, Ohio, area, including northern Kentucky.*

The following viewpoint is the text of a report that appeared during the 1850s in the Cincinnati Enquirer, *providing details of the event Toni Morrison used as the basis of* Beloved. *A party of slaves escaped from Kentucky to Ohio, where slavery was unlawful. Their former slave owners arrived in Ohio to capture them and return them to slavery, the newspaper reports. Instead of allowing her children to return to slavery, a young mother kills her infant. This incident raises considerable controversy, the newspaper says, with some calling it murder while abolitionists regard the mother as a heroine.*

The city was thrown into much excitement yesterday morning by the information that a party of slaves, sixteen in all, had made a stampede from Kentucky to this side of the river. Other circumstances, however, which afterward transpired, have imparted a degree of horrible interest to the affair different to that which usually attends a stampede of negroes.

Reclaiming Runaway Slaves

The particulars are as follows: Three of the slaves, who bore the relationship of father, mother and son, the two former apparently about fifty years of age, the son twenty-five, were the property of Mr. James Marshall, of Richwood Station, Boone County, about sixteen miles back of Covington, and five oth-

Cincinnati Enquirer, "Stampede of Slaves: A Tale of Horror," January 29, 1856. Reproduced by permission.

ers, consisting of a woman named Peggy and her four children, the oldest about five years of age, the youngest an infant at the breast, belonging to Mr. Archibald K. Gaines, who resided in the immediate vicinity of Mr. Marshall. Peggy was married to young Simon, the slave of Mr. Marshall, and the son of the old couple with whom he ran away.

It seems that about ten o'clock on Sunday night the party took a pair of horses and a sleigh, belonging to Mr. Marshall, with which they drove to Covington, where they left the team standing outside of the Washington House, where it was found by the landlord, the horses very much blown [winded] from the severe manner in which they had been driven. In the meantime the party of eight crossed the river on the ice and took refuge in a house, the fourth below Millcreek bridge, tenanted by a negro named Kite, a son of old Joe Kite, well known for years in this city. Young Kite was well acquainted with the parties, for he has himself lived in their neighborhood, having been formerly owned there, but his freedom was purchased some time since by his father.

Early yesterday morning, Mr. Gaines, accompanied by a son of Mr. Marshall, arrived in this city in pursuit of the fugitives.

Application was made to United States Commissioner Penders, who thereupon issued his warrant, which was placed in the hands of the United States Marshal, who, having received information of the hiding place of the fugitives, collected a posse of officers, some from Kentucky and others belonging to this city, and with Mr. Gaines, Mr. Marshall, Jr., and Major Murphy, who accompanied them from Richwood, they proceeded to the residence of Kite.

Arrived there they found the doors and windows fastened, but upon thundering at the door, Kite looked out of a window and at first agreed to admit them, but afterward refused to do so, and at this juncture, as they were about to force an entrance, young Simon fired from the window with a revolver, the ball from which struck the finger of one of the deputized marshals, named John Patterson, and then lodged in his upper lip, leaving the finger hanging by a mere thread.

Upon this the door was burst in, when Simon fired three more shots at the party, fortunately, however, without [any] taking effect. Mr. Gaines seized him by the wrist and wrenched the pistol from his hand before he could [shoot] the other two barrels off, it being a six-shooter.

A Baby Killed

But a deed of horror had been consummated, for weltering in its blood, the throat being cut from ear to ear and the head almost severed from the body, upon the floor lay one of the children of the younger couple, a girl three years old, while in a back room, crouched beneath the bed, two more of the children, boys, of two and five years, were moaning, the one having received two gashes in its throat, the other a cut upon the head.

As the party entered the room the mother was seen wielding a heavy shovel, and before she could be secured she inflicted a heavy blow with it upon the face of the infant, which was lying upon the floor. The whole party having been arrested, medical aid was procured for the little sufferers, whose wounds were not of a fatal character, and then all were carried to the office of the United States Marshal, when United States Commissioner Pendery fixed the hearing of the case for this morning at nine o'clock.

Coroner Menzies immediately hastened to the spot where the dead body of the child was found, and summoned a jury, when, after examining five of the parties who first burst into the house, not one of whom, however, could throw any light as to whether the father or mother of the child had committed the bloody deed, the further hearing of the testimony was postponed until this morning.

The only information derived from the eldest boy, in reply to who had injured him and the other children, is that the folks in the house did it. When taken to the office of the United States Marshal, the woman declared that they had received their wounds in the melee which followed the entrance of the posse into the house, but this is known to be untrue. The fearful act lies between one or the other of the miserable parents, perhaps both, but doubtless, the truth will be brought out by the Coroner to-day.

The old couple are mild and rather intelligent in their appearance; the mother of the children is a good-looking, hearty negress, while her husband bears the appearance of having been well cared for, in fact, young Mr. Marshall states that he has always treated him more as a companion than a slave; they have been playmates in childhood and have grown up together, "And now," said he, "if money can save him from the effect of any rash act he has committed I am willing to give it to any amount."

Murderer or Heroine?

After the United States Commissioner had adjourned the hearing of the case until this morning, a couple of hackney coaches were procured for conveying the fugitives to the Hammond-street Station-house, but a crowd was assembled in the street, whose threats alarmed the hackmen for the safety of their carriages, and the prisoners were accordingly walked under the conduct of a strong escort. Some threats were made by a portion of the mob, but no violence or attempt at rescue was made; subsequently, they were lodged for safer keeping in the County Jail.

In the meantime, the leading Abolitionists busied themselves, and a writ of habeas corpus was procured, commanding the United States Marshal to produce the fugitives before Judge Burgoyne of the Probate Court; they, however, were allowed to remain in Jail, and will be brought before the United States Commissioner, as previously arranged.

At the time of the flight of Messrs., Gaines and Marshall's negroes, a gang of eight left Covington, six belonging to Mr. Levi F. Dougherty, five men and one woman, and two men owned by John W. Stevenson, Esq., both residents of Covington. The Marshal of Covington, with several officers of this city, supposed they were upon their track, but after a fruitless search, they found themselves at fault, and at a late hour last night no clue had been obtained of their lurking place.

In the meantime there is much excitement existing, the bloody episode having invested the affair with a tinge of fearful, although romantic interest. The Abolitionists regard the parents of the murdered child as a hero and heroine, teeming with lofty and holy emotions, who, Virginiuslike[1] would rather imbue their hands in the blood of their offspring than allow them to wear the shackles of slavery, while others look upon them as brutal and unnatural murderers.

At any rate, the affair will furnish some employment to lawyers as well as officers, as extra force for the latter being necessary to prevent rescue while the case is pending.

1. In Chaucer's "Physician's Tale," one of his *Canterbury Tales*, the protagonist Virginius, an ancient Roman, beheads his daughter rather than let her suffer the forced loss of her chastity to a corrupt official.

Social Issues in Literature

CHAPTER 2

Slavery in *Beloved*

Beloved Shows How the Power of Love Helped Black People Survive Slavery

Carolyn C. Denard

Carolyn C. Denard is on the graduate faculty of Emory University in Atlanta, Georgia.

In the following excerpt, Denard explains how she teaches Beloved *to her students. The overwhelming reaction many white students have on reading* Beloved *is guilt, while many black students experience anger, she states. In Denard's opinion, to understand Toni Morrison's intent in writing the book, they must get beyond these emotions. Morrison's theme is that despite the horrors of slavery, many black people led meaningful lives enriched by their love for each other.*

This essay addresses a series of responses that I have received from students over the past few years while teaching Toni Morrison's *Beloved*. I must explain at the outset that most of the students to whom I have taught the novel have been white. And what has struck me and created a moment of pedagogical pause, as a black woman professor, has been the students' seemingly paralyzing responses of guilt, embarrassment, and hurt. Students have said quietly to me after reading this novel, "How can you even *look* at me after reading this novel?" As some students have accepted personally the blame for the atrocities in this novel, others have expressed everything from cavalier rejection of the awful ways of the whites in *Beloved* to tearful and apologetic "I didn't know"s as they have claimed contemporary distancing from their ancestors.

Carolyn C. Denard, *Approaches to Teaching the Novels of Toni Morrison.* New York, NY: The Modern Language Association of America, 1997. Reproduced by permission of the Modern Language Association of America.

Black students, too, have been caught up in the horrifying historical events of this text, and while they have not expressed guilt or apology, they have had equally paralyzing responses of anger and disbelief—at the treatment of the slaves and at both the ghost and the killing of the child. In my decision to address these responses from students pedagogically, I am not trying to minimize them or smooth over the awful history unfolded in this text: good literature should change our vision and call on us to speak out; good literature should elicit passionate response.

Not About the Evils of Slavery

But what I have worried about as a teacher of *Beloved* is the obstacle these apologies, this fear, this guilt, and this anger present for students—if they do not move beyond these emotional responses to get at the larger message of the novel. I do not want students to walk away from the novel, as some are prone to do when confronted with the historical realities it presents, and to translate it into a pathological rendering of slavery, told to inform them of the barbarity of the slave masters and the slave mothers. And while I believe some guilt-ridden or angry revelations are healthy and necessary, I am troubled by the cowering deference of mostly white students to these first responses: they lie down for their beating, they shut up, they agree. They don't dare question or challenge me or the text. I am concerned that by adopting this posture toward the racial history, which is certainly a true and major part of the story, they will not learn that it is on the back of this horrifying history of slavery that Morrison makes her eloquent and hopeful thematic statement in the novel. I am concerned that they will be too consumed with nursing their wounds to see how the text sets straight the record of black life and black humanity during slavery.

A novelist addresses a question similar to that of the cultural anthropologist. If history is what happened, then literature—or, for the anthropologist, ethnography—is what what happened *means*. There are many documentable historical facts in *Beloved*: the story of Margaret Garner, the cruelty of life on slave plantations, the inhumanity of the Middle Passage, and the trials and triumphs of the Underground Railroad.

But that history is not the sum total of the story Morrison tells in this novel. She seeks to get at the interior of that history, to see how these awful experiences, historically lumped into statistical summaries of the slave experience, affected slaves one by one. Students need to be reminded that their initial discomfort is a response to the historically based facts of the text—or, as [critic] Clifford Geertz would say, to the "thin description" of the text. They must understand that Morrison's rendering of that history in human terms—the enhancing, imaginative interpretation of that history—is the real test of the merit of the novel. In an interview with Mervyn Rothstein, Morrison says:

> The novel is not about slavery. Slavery is very predictable. There it is and there's [information] about how it is, and then you get out of it or you don't. [The novel] can't be driven by slavery. It has to be the interior life of some people, and everything that they do is impacted on by the horror of slavery, but they, are also people.

How Slaves Survived Is Important

What Morrison is after and what thick description seeks to articulate, then, is the meaning of history on a human level for those who experienced these horrors one by one.

To get at that interior life, Morrison relies on a sensitive and trusting imagination, on her kinship with other human beings, and on a haunting ancestral memory. Sethe's killing of her child in *Beloved* is based on the story of a slave woman, Margaret Garner, who killed one of her children and tried to kill the rest to prevent them from being returned to slavery. Morrison said that after reading Garner's story

> I didn't do any more research at all about that story. I did a lot of research about everything else in the book—Cincinnati, and abolitionists, and the Underground Railroad—but I refused to find out anything else about Margaret Garner. I really wanted to invent her life.

In teaching *Beloved*, then, I try to help students focus not so much on the historical background of the novel (slavery) as on the human, interactive foreground of the novel (how people survived). Students find it easiest to concentrate on the historical background in this aesthetically and thematically complex novel because that is what they are most familiar with, even if only in a cursory way. They know that slavery existed, that it was wrong, and that it was a scourge on individuals and the nation. As teachers, we must help students to look beyond that history and to focus more carefully on the black men and women trying to carry out meaningful, human lives after slavery, which bruised and bloodied their humanity but did not destroy it. We must give students the tools—questions, sensitive analyses, role-playing exercises—that they need to change their perception of the novel.

I discuss here two tools I have used to help students change their angle of vision in reading *Beloved*. The first tool is a cultural analysis of the characters' responses to history. Analyzing these responses foregrounds the community of ex-slaves and helps students focus on the values held by the blacks themselves as agents of their own humanity rather than as resigned victims of the values of their white enslavers. The second tool is a series of questions in which students analyze their responses to historical events and compare them with the characters'. The questions allow the students to address the history outright, but also the questions lead the students to examine the individual human responses to history. In my classes I always begin with the questions, but I offer the analysis here first so that readers will better understand the context and the thematic direction of the questions.

Love Defines Humanity

The largest portion of the self-defining humanity of the black characters in *Beloved*, surprisingly enough in a world filled with hatred, is their manifestations of love—thick love, tiny love, jealous love, thirty-mile love, self-love, family love, community love—the modification of it, the protection from it, the overindulgence in it, the guardedness of it, the insistence on it. Loving the self, the family, the friend, the child, the natural world becomes a balm for the horror of slavery. In the foreground of this text is a story of the varying ways in which a people tries to impart human love in inhuman times.

Sethe's motivation before and after the killing of her child is a desire to love:

> I was big, Paul D, and deep and wide and when I stretched out my arms all my children could get in between. I was *that* wide. Look like I loved em more after I got there. Or maybe I couldn't love em proper in Kentucky because they wasn't mine to love. But when I got here, when I jumped down off that wagon—there wasn't nobody in the world I couldn't love if I wanted to.

Paul D is also motivated by love. He keeps his sanity and his humanity intact when confined to a chain gang in Alfred, Georgia, by continuing and protecting, if only in a small way, his ability to love: "[Y]ou protected yourself and loved small. Picked the tiniest star out of the sky to own; lay down with head twisted in order to see the loved one over the rim of the trench before you slept."

Baby Suggs, because of her knowledge of the power of love and her insistence on imparting that knowledge to others, takes it as the text for her memorable sermon in the clearing:

"Here," she said, "in this place, we flesh; flesh that weeps, laughs; flesh that dances on bare feet in grass. Love it. Love it hard. . . . Love your hands! Love them. Raise them up and kiss them. Touch others with them, pat them together, stroke them on your face 'cause they don't love that either. *You* got to love it! . . ."

There are other examples: Denver's love for Beloved, Sixo's love for the Thirty-Mile Woman, Halle's love for Baby Suggs. The novel progressively becomes a story about the ability, the willingness of those who were not beloved, to love.

A Code of Ethics Was Important

The other manifestation of the characters' humanity, and to my mind the bravest and most remarkable example of Morrisons ability to represent her characters on their own terms, is their ability to claim their own guilt and in turn seek their own forgiveness with one another. Their sense of guilt is not put forth in language dependent on or relative to the destructive and immoral slave system that whites leveled against blacks daily. It is established according to the codes of behavior that blacks, despite this system, set forth as right and acceptable for themselves.

If *Beloved* were written just to criticize a system that subjected a group of human beings to inhuman treatment, Morrison would not need to show the code of ethics among the oppressed group. But Morrison does, and though the horror of slavery seems a reasonable cause for a violation of ethics, it does not exempt from punishment the violators of the community's code. Nor does it exempt them from their personal need to repent and ask for forgiveness. Indeed, much of the present-time focus of the story concerns the characters' working out, or facing the consequences of violating, their own codes.

Cast members Thandie Newton (Beloved), Danny Glover (Paul D), Oprah Winfrey (Sethe), and Beah Richards (Baby Suggs, seated) at the premiere of the film version of Beloved *on October 12, 1998, in Los Angeles.* © Fred Prouser/Reuters/Landov.

The community, feeling Baby Suggs is too prosperous, too prideful, does not warn her and the others of the coming of strangers:

Nobody warned them, and [Stamp Paid had] always believed it wasn't the exhaustion from a long day's gorging
that dulled them, but some other thing—like, well, like
meanness—that let them stand aside, or not pay attention,
or tell themselves somebody else was probably bearing the
news already to the house on Bluestone Road. . . .

Believing Sethe's actions are too extreme and her response to
the deed irreverent and arrogant, the community ostracizes
her for "trying to do it all alone with her nose in the air." Ella,
Sethe's most vocal critic in the community, "understood Sethe's
rage in the shed twenty years ago, but not her reaction to it,
which Ella thought was prideful, misdirected, and Sethe herself too complicated." Even Paul D believes that Sethe's killing
of the baby was beneath her: "'You got two feet, Sethe, not
four.'" And Baby Suggs is depressed to her death by the overwhelming contradiction of Sethe's action: "[S]he could not
approve or condemn Sethe's rough choice. One or the other
might have saved her, but beaten up by the claims of both, she
went to bed." And finally Sethe herself risks self-destruction as
she repents and seeks forgiveness from the ghost of her daughter: "I won't never let her go. I'll explains to her. . . . Why I did
it. How if I hadn't killed her she would have died and that is
something I could not bear to happen to her. When I explain
it she'll understand. . . . I'll tend her as no mother ever tended
a child . . ."

The community members must not only face their guilt
over the death of the baby but also work out their terms for
forgiveness—for themselves and for Sethe. Denver comes to
realize that even the ghost has gone too far in violating a
daughter's respect for her mother and finally brings the conflict to a halt with a cry for help: "Somebody had to be
saved. . . . Nobody was going to help her unless she told it—
told all of it." And when Ella hears Denver's story, she too
agrees that Beloved's actions have surpassed what is reasonable and acceptable in the community—even for a ghost:

Whatever Sethe had done, Ella didn't like the idea of past errors taking possession of the present. Sethe's crime was staggering and her pride outstripped even that; but she could not countenance the possibility of sin moving on in the house, unleashed and sassy.... She didn't mind a little communication between the two worlds, but this was an invasion.

Determined to restore the moral order in the community, Ella leads a group of thirty neighborhood women in prayer to the house on Bluestone Road to exorcise the ghost and offer Sethe forgiveness.

All these characters are motivated in their anger, their guilt, and their forgiveness by the black community's code of ethics. Slavery gets none of them off the hook, and they must answer to themselves and their community before they finally achieve forgiveness and are able to move forward.

This is the powerful subject of the novel: How a people try to keep their humanity intact in a world whose morality and humanity is turned upside down—and how they succeed. If students are too consumed with abhorring the history revealed in the text and, thus, do not pay attention to the novel's depiction of the power and endurance of the effort to claim one's humanity, then they miss the larger, more important message.

The Human Meaning of the Facts

I initially developed the following list of hypothetical questions to sensitize students to the human meaning behind the historical facts of this novel, and I suggest it now as an early discussion exercise to encourage students to respond not only to the history but, more important, to the characters' responses to that history.

You have a choice of killing your baby or allowing it to grow up in a system that defines it as chattel and freely sells, rapes, beats it without allowing it any opportunity for defiance. What do you do? (Because some students find this situation hard to imagine, I sometimes use the following one instead: You are a political prisoner. You have been subject to the worst, most inhumane treatment imaginable. You escape with your young child. You are captured. You can either kill the child or have the child live the life that you have lived. What do you do?)

A woman in your community kills her children to save them from what, in her opinion, is a living hell. How do you, as a community member, respond?

You are on the jury in Sethe's trial. Given the circumstances of the death as described in the novel, how do you judge her? Why?

You are an adult heterosexual male deprived of normal, healthy sexual relationships with women year after year after year. You cannot leave your situation, and you are only in the company of other men. What do you do? What do you do to the persons who impose this life on you?

You are sent away to a work camp where you receive treatment worse than slavery, and you are at the mercy of the overseers sexual and physical whims. What do you do?

You are chained and a heavy iron bit is placed in your mouth, strapping your tongue and keeping you open-mouthed yet silent for days or weeks. What do you do? How do you feel after the ordeal is over?

I get a full range of answers: "I would kill my child." "I would fight back." "I would try to help her." "I would acquit the woman." "I would run away." "I would just die." "I would pray for deliverance." "I don't know what I would do." It is a good role-playing exercise, even with its inherent role-playing limitations of pretense. It allows the students to respond immediately to the historical issues that bother them. It also allows for an instructive comparison of their responses with the characters' when we discuss the novel later.

I try to keep the responses and the ensuing discussion as serious and focused as possible. Some students overstate their responses for laughs, but I always take them back to the point of the question, trying to elicit their most basic human responses.

The only student response that is usually similar to a character's involves the killing of the child. Many students disagree with this option, but most see it as heroic. What is interesting is that this response is precisely the one for which Sethe has to pay and of which the community disapproves. Even though Morrison, as the "defense," presents a case that seems to justify the action, it is also the action for which Sethe pays throughout most of the novel. Herein lies the complexity of the novel, a complexity that this role playing allows students to ponder.

This exercise also boosts serious character analysis; it pushes students closer toward making thematic statements about the meaning of the novel on many levels. For both black and white students the history becomes more a means of understanding the development of strength and complexity of character than an end in itself.

A Tribute to the Human Spirit

One thing that becomes clear to students after this exercise is how the killing of the baby affects Sethe. Even though she is glad to have saved her daughter from slavery, her grief and guilt nearly destroy her as she seeks forgiveness. The students come to realize the complexity of Sethe's decision. They have argued about it; they have put themselves in her place. They have seen Sethe save her children from Sweet Home and understand the protective logic of her action, but they also understand that she pays for the decision on a personal, moral level. They understand that Morrison has not allowed slavery to destroy Sethe's human ability for love *or* for guilt. They better understand Morrison when she says of Sethe's action:

"[Sethe] did the right thing but she didn't have the right to do it." It is a powerful moment for students when they begin to reflect on the political and moral implications of Sethe's decision.

What also becomes clear to students, once they have been encouraged to focus on how individuals respond to their historical circumstances rather than just on the history itself, is the enduring and indomitable nature of the human spirit. Morrison's imaginative re-creation here is not just her fantasy. She is trying to explain in human terms what did exist. How a people subjected to the most inhuman form of treatment, the most hateful, love-defying existence, kept their human potential for both love and guilt intact. That is why despite hundreds of years of bestial, inhumane treatment blacks are still living basically humane, loving lives. Morrison tells us this history to show us the power of love in spite of it. She wants her readers to understand that while blacks were often driven to excess by the cruelties of slavery, slavery was not allowed to excuse those actions.

Both black and white students can use the code of ethics revealed in the development of the black community in this text as a representative example of the best that is human in the individual. As students are made to examine the lives of these "victims" of history within the moral and spiritual structure of the lives that the characters determined for themselves, students might begin to see this novel not as an exercise in self-flagellation or an opportunity to rekindle anger but as a call to triumph over the misery, the unfairness, the bitterness of history in their own lives and bring forth their "best thing[s]", their best human selves. For as Morrison has shown in the writing of *Beloved*, what lies beyond the bitterness of the history revealed in this novel is a people trying desperately, triumphantly, dangerously even, to forgive and to love.

Morrison Uses Slave Songs to Show the Humanity of Slaves

Peter J. Capuano

Peter J. Capuano is an assistant professor in the English Department at the University of Nebraska–Lincoln.

According to Capuano in the following article, authors of traditional slave narratives were compelled to downplay the emotional impact of slave songs to avoid offending a white audience. Contemporary writers are not constrained by this concern, Capuano explains. In Beloved, *Toni Morrison permits the full emotional impact of slave songs, with their stories of the atrocities of slavery, to come through, the author suggests. For Morrison, slave songs were how slaves affirmed their humanity in a hostile environment, Capuano maintains.*

In her 1987 novel *Beloved*, Toni Morrison acknowledges and even borrows from Frederick Douglass's 1845 *Narrative [of the Life of Frederick Douglass: An American Slave]*, but she also makes a resolute break from its rhetorical and political objectives. Historical differences between the audiences of Douglass and Morrison account for a large part of their contrasting styles, particularly in their treatment of slave song. Since Douglass composed his *Narrative* as a fugitive slave in the early 1840s, he was aware of his principally white audience and also of his precarious task of presenting an attack not on white America, but on the institution of slavery itself. Douglass's judicious decision to report the bleakness of slavery with austerity of tone allows him to present this attack successfully. He

Peter J. Capuano, "Truth in Timbre: Morrison's Extension of Slave Narrative Song in Beloved," *African American Review*, vol. 37, Spring 2003, p. 95. Reproduced by permission of the author.

relies heavily on factual evidence, rather than on the tremendously emotional slave songs, to present the most appalling scenes of brutality endured by the slaves in his narrative.

This shrewd emphasis on the factual enables Douglass to navigate between the specific facts and the general nature of slavery in a way that informs rather than offends his audience. In 1845 Douglass could not afford to focus repeatedly on the "ineffable sadness" of slave songs or on the songs' reflection of "souls boiling over with the bitterest anguish," even though he reports early in the *Narrative* that "every tone [is] a testimony against slavery." . . . Douglass's task of uncovering the truth of slavery's brutality without mitigating that truth with indignant protestations has proven to be at once inhibiting and fecund. The awareness of this predicament limits his treatment of slave song in the 1845 *Narrative*, but it also creates a colossal paradigm of song's importance for many contemporary authors such as Toni Morrison and Charles Johnson, who explore similar topics.

Morrison's Use of Slave Song

Morrison's *Beloved* responds deliberately and exhaustively to the description of slave song that appears at the outset of Douglass's 1845 *Narrative*. The fact that Morrison is not inhibited by the pressing need to abolish slavery allows her to explore the specificity of the slave songs to a degree that Douglass simply could not risk in 1845. The essential goal of Douglass's *Narrative* in 1845 was to inform what [writer and abolitionist] William Lloyd Garrison dubbed a "stubbornly incredulous" white audience of slavery's politically sanctioned barbarity. Since Morrison is not inhibited by the socio-political exigencies taken on by Douglass, she is free to focus more on song as a point of access into the reverberating effects of slavery's horrors—the same horrors that Douglass relates to his readers with a conspicuous deficit of emotion. The project of Morrison's novel is to register and index the vital relationship between the "personhood" of African Americans and the specific songs of former slaves. This is to say that the original description of slave song in Douglass, looming in the background of Morrison's novel, shapes her handling of music and song, her insistence on its signal importance as an indicator of human status in *Beloved*.

Morrison's consistent but subtle use of song takes the reader beyond the horrifying facts of Douglass's narrative and into the more profoundly emotional turmoil of a post-emancipation community. Morrison reverses the traditional slave narrative format and expands the scope of the reader's comprehension by investigating a crime committed by the oppressed rather than by the oppressor. Through her exploration of the black experience within slavery and beyond, Morrison shows how song defines and affirms slave "personhood" in a world where slave humanity is constantly challenged and denied. Morrison's treatment of song in *Beloved* provides the reader with a testimony that is significantly different from the testimonies set forth in the slave narratives. Morrison's testimony does not end with the establishment of slavery's barbarity; it chronicles her characters' endurance and ability to survive during and after these periods of physical brutality and psychological abuse. The principal characters of the novel— Sethe, Paul D, and Sixo—all associate song with their humanity and use it as a shield against indignity and despair. In this way, Morrison relies on the rubric of the "sorrow songs" from Frederick Douglass's 1845 *Narrative* in *Beloved* to challenge a contemporary audience to recognize slave humanity beyond the simple (but no less important) acknowledgment of slavery's brutality.

Song Is a Way of Affirming Humanity

Often in *Beloved*, when characters cannot read or write or even talk about the brutality they experience as slaves, they sing to affirm their participation in life and defend their status as human beings. Song offers slaves the opportunity to express their personal testimonies while remaining within the framework of their larger cultural experiences—all without actually speaking of their shame and trauma. . . . The slaves of *Beloved* defend their personhood and revive their endurance when it is challenged and violated by "mossy teeth," numerical measurements, and leg irons. For these reasons, it is fitting that Sethe characterizes Paul D, a man who endures enormous physical and psychological abuse, as a "singing man" at the outset of the novel.

Traditionally, critics have either ignored song as a legitimate vehicle for establishing slave humanity or have limited their appraisal of song. Margaret Atwood [in "Haunted by Their Nightmares"] notes how the theme of "tyrannical price" runs through *Beloved* but stops short of offering analysis of how slaves combat this tyranny with song and re-establish their humanity by singing about life. The slaves of *Beloved* have their humanity stripped from them throughout the novel, as cold statisticians like Schoolteacher attempt to calculate and record their "animal" tendencies above and beyond their "human" characteristics. In one such instance, Paul D learns "the dollar value of his weight, his strength, his heart, his brain, his penis, and his future" but responds by singing of the "bosses and masters and misses; of mules and dogs and the shamelessness of life" in order to confirm his humanity in the face of Schoolteacher's dehumanizing "value" equations.

Song Is Key to Survival

With Morrison's *Beloved*, we hear the spoken stories of Paul D, Sixo, Baby Suggs, and Sethe, and we are also aware of their songs that bear witness to the unspeakable horrors of slavery—those experiences whose shame transcends even the spoken word.

Whereas Douglass cites the importance of slave song for the first and last time at the end of his narrative's second chapter, Morrison establishes song as imperative to her characters' survival during nearly every chapter of *Beloved*. She includes the ability to sing among the barest and most rudimentary essentials of human existence early in the novel. At the house on Bluestone Road, if Paul D could "walk, eat, sleep, [and] sing," he could survive and "asked for no more." Morrison also has Paul D sing while he mends "things he had broken the day before," in an effort to reconstruct his life after physical and emotional trials have shattered his identity at prison camp in Alfred, Georgia. Morrison emphasizes the importance of singing to Paul D's survival through her repeated acknowledgment at the outset of the novel that his songs "were too loud [and] had too much power for the little house chores he was engaged in." In reality, Paul D's songs help him to reconstruct the broken pieces of his past life in Georgia more than to reset and glaze the table at 124 Bluestone Road.

The songs that Paul D sings upon his arrival at Sethe's house solidify both his autonomous and his collective participation in the black experience of slavery. On the individual level, Paul D "change[s] the words," "throwing in a line if one occur[s] to him" to establish an element of personal testimony in the song. In this crucial depiction of Paul D's singing, Morrison actually invokes the paradigm of song established by Frederick Douglass at the end of his narrative's second chapter:

> The slaves selected to go to the Great House Farm, for the monthly allowance for themselves and their fellow-slaves, were peculiarly enthusiastic. While on their way, they would make the dense old woods, for many miles around, reverberate with their wild songs, revealing at once the highest joy and the deepest sadness. They would compose and sing as they went along, consulting neither time nor tune. The thought that came up, came out—if not in the word, in the sound;—and as frequently in one as in the other. They would sometimes sing the most pathetic sentiment in the

most rapturous tone, and the most rapturous sentiment in the most pathetic tone. Into all of their songs they would manage to weave something of the Great House Farm. . . . They would sing, as a chorus, to words which to many would seem unmeaning jargon, but which, nevertheless, were full of meaning to themselves.

In this way, slaves could bring their singular experiences to a song without relation to anyone else. On the other hand, song allows the slaves an opportunity to participate in the larger history of the black experience of shame, suffering, and endurance. If the thought did not come out in Paul D's individual word, it came out in the tone of the song. Therefore, by changing the lines of the songs he sings at 124, Paul D establishes the autonomy of his particular experience while affirming his participation in and his endurance of the institution of slavery. It is interesting to note that, as her character Paul D accomplishes this, Morrison aligns *Beloved* within a tradition larger (and more important) than its Pulitzer Prize scope: the troping of song in American slave narratives. The specificity of Paul D's songs later in *Beloved*, though, exposes a primary difference between Morrison and Douglass. Douglass establishes the crucial relationship between slaves and their songs, but Morrison probes deeper into the specifics of this relationship.

Song Helps Combat Despair

The cryptic nature of Paul D's character provides a particularly apposite site for Morrison to begin the process of extending Douglass's paradigm. Paul D's most gruesome experience occurs while under the supervision of Schoolteacher at Sweet Home, after Mr. Garner's death. Because of Schoolteacher's empirical (but no less brutal) division of "slaves" and "humans," and because he announces himself "with a coach full of paper" to record these discrepancies, [critic] Rafael Perez-Torres accurately suggests [in "Between Presence and Absence: *Beloved*, Postmodernism, and Black-

Frederick Douglass, photographed around the time he published his 1845 autobiography,
Narrative of the Life of Frederick Douglass, an American Slave. © Bettmann/Corbis.

ness"] that Schoolteacher "becomes the speaking subject of slavery's discourse." Paul D's dehumanizing experience with Schoolteacher is so physically and psychologically grueling that he has "never talked about it" and never "told a soul." In one of the most solemn episodes of the novel, Paul D confides to Sethe that he could never speak to anyone about having his "tongue held down by iron" while looking at the roosters who had more freedom "to be and stay" than he. . . .

Paul D's horrific experience at prison camp in Georgia is an episode in which Morrison shows the power of song to combat even the worst and most dehumanizing despair. Song in *Beloved* not only "mends broken things," but it also gives Paul D the endurance to survive the chain gang in Georgia, where his humanity is aggressively violated. Paul D uses song to defend his humanity when it is denied most by "wooden boxes," "cage doors," "leg irons," and "bit[s] of foreskin." As Morrison notes, "The songs from Georgia were flatheaded nails for pounding and pounding and pounding." These songs give Paul D the strength to brook eighty-six days of pounding rock and eighty-six nights while "reaching for air." Most notably, as Paul D and other prisoners "danc[ed] two-step to the music of hand-forged iron," they sang to affirm their humanity while being worked and tied like animals.

> They sang of the women they knew; the children they had been; the animals they had tamed themselves or seen others tame. They sang of bosses and masters and misses; of mules and dogs and the shamelessness of life. They sang lovingly of graveyards and sisters long gone. Of pork in the woods; meal in the pan; fish on the line; cane, rain and rocking chairs.

Morrison's inclusion of the specific topics of the slave songs from Georgia allows the reader to identify more closely with incredibly complex ideas of identity and worth during and after the chattel experience. She extends the concept of "weaving" from Douglass's description of the Great House Farm songs to include the specific song topics. The emphasis on the "animal" in these particular songs allows the slaves in Georgia's prison camp to establish themselves as human beings capable of acknowledging their humanity, even when their oppressors refuse to do the same. By singing about mules and dogs, pork and fish, relationships and pleasures, the slaves assert their humanity and defend themselves against the atrocities of the camp. Perhaps most importantly, Morrison's specific exploration of song reveals how "the men got through" chattel slavery and its horrifying reverberations even after emancipation. . . .

Slavery Hurt Both Master and Slave

Sound alone registers the humanity of *Beloved*'s slaves most incisively when Schoolteacher captures Paul A, Paul D, Sixo, and the Thirty-Mile Woman as they attempt to escape from slavery at Sweet Home. Caught and facing death by firing squad for their bold transgression, Sixo "grabs the mouth of the nearest pointing rifle" and "begins to sing." The white men find it impossible to shoot Sixo as he sings because the song locates "personhood" among slavery for a group of slave catchers who are conditioned to see only the "animals" of Schoolteacher's calculations. Slave catchers are trained to kill animals in leg irons with bits in their mouths—not human beings singing songs. Morrison acknowledges this discrepancy as the white men wait "with five guns trained on [Sixo] while they listen" to his song. Realizing that his song makes him far too human to shoot, one white man finally "hits Sixo in the head" to make him stop singing. Ironically, Schoolteacher changes his mind about wanting Sixo alive; his song must have convinced Schoolteacher "that he was too human ever to become a docile slave." Only after Sixo "is through with his song" do the white men see a slave and proceed to burn him alive.

[Former slave and abolitionist] Henry Bibb and Frederick Douglass refer to the institution of slavery as "the man destroying system" in their narratives, and Morrison tropes this idea of universal human degradation in *Beloved*. Morrison's revision of the traditional slave narrative comes, though, as she offers song as a response to the degradation.

Just as Captain Auld, Mrs. Auld, and Mr. Covey are rendered less human by the effects of their association with slavery, so too are the white characters in Morrison's novel. As [critic] Houston A. Baker, Jr., points out [in *Long Black Song: Essays in Black American Literature and Culture*], "Douglass is aware of American slavery's chattel principle, which equated slaves with livestock, and he is not reluctant to employ animal metaphors to capture the general inhumanity of the system." Morrison shows how Schoolteacher and the slave catchers from *Beloved* act with the same barbarity and inhuman cruelty that epitomizes slave treatment during the chattel experience of the slave narrative. Because they are involved in what Douglass calls the "soul-killing" business of keeping slaves, Schoolteacher and the other white men of *Beloved* are reduced to subhuman behavior. Morrison derives this principle of categorical human degradation from Douglass's *Narrative*. As Baker points out, slavery has a uniquely pernicious identity resulting from its power to degrade all it touches:

> Douglass's work is a chronicle of the "soul-killing" effect slavery had on both master and slave. Time and time again in the *Narrative* men's hopes for a better life are crushed: humans are whipped and slaughtered like animals; men and women are changed into maniacal and sadistic creatures by power; the strength of body and mind is destroyed by an avaricious and degrading system.

Morrison's *Beloved*, however, does not simply chronicle the degradation set in motion by slavery; the novel also reveals how slaves use song to combat the inhuman protocol adopted by the oppressors. In this way, Morrison compels her audience to acknowledge the draconian punishment for an "offense" that needs no hyperbole—the act of burning alive a singing man who tries to escape a life of slavery.

Sixo establishes his humanity in front of the white men with his song, and the fact that Morrison does not record the words of this song is testimony to the higher significance of its sound. With Paul D's misunderstanding of the words to Sixo's song, Morrison shows the reader how the words to slave songs are belittled by the content of their sound. Her awareness of the precision with which Douglass locates the arresting inadequacy of these "would be" words is crucial to Morrison's project with sound in *Beloved*. Douglass reports early in his narrative: "I have sometimes thought that the mere hearing of those songs would do more to impress some minds with the horrible character of slavery, than the reading of whole volumes of philosophy on the subject could do." Caught by Schoolteacher and the slave catchers, Paul D thinks he should have sung something loud and rolling to go with Sixo's tune, but the words put him off—he didn't "understand the words." By including this information, Morrison establishes the slave song as the ultimate projection of the human experience—one where words have no meaning and the sound carries every inch of sorrow and despair harbored inside the members of the enslaved community. . . .

Song and Sethe's Forgiveness

Morrison also explores the complex relationship between song and humanity with her depiction of Beloved's unique origin—the events that surround Sethe's murder of her own child. She shifts song's function slightly to accommodate Sethe's unusual isolation from her own people. With Paul D and Sixo, Morrison's use of song defends the personhood of slaves, but with Sethe, song defines and affirms the neighborhood's decision to banish her. Immediately after murdering her daughter Beloved, Sethe exits through "a throng of black faces" but with no "cape of sound to hold and steady her on her way." The crucial absence of song highlights the fact that even Sethe's black neighbors regard her as inhuman for having murdered her own child. If Sethe had acted less barbarically, her personhood would have been recognized by the spectators and "the singing would have begun at once." Also, Morrison juxtaposes Sethe's seeming inhumanity with the "creatures" and "cannibals" that are mentioned on the pages immediately preceding Sethe's emergence from the house on Bluestone Road. In the same way that the "four horsemen" regard the slaves as having "gone wild," Morrison's choice to omit song in this episode shows how Sethe's own people believe her to be somehow less than human. The black neighbors wait until the cart carrying Sethe "head[s] west" before they make any sound at all. This conspicuous deficiency of song reveals the neighborhood consensus of Sethe's barbarity and ultimately signifies her formal banishment from the community.

On the other hand, Morrison uses the prevalence of song at the end of the novel to re-establish Sethe's humanity. After supporting a twenty-year policy of banishment from the neighborhood, the women in Sethe's community begin to question their harsh treatment and wonder about the "killed one" (Beloved) who has suddenly reappeared in the flesh. Ella, a deeply compassionate woman who had been "shared by husband and son" during puberty, finally convinces the other women that "rescue [from banishment i]s in order" for Sethe. Ella manages to persuade the others that "the idea of past errors taking control of the present" is an unjust burden on another human being and "so thirty women walk slowly, slowly toward 124." Morrison reinstates song here to reflect the change in the neighbor women's assessment of Sethe's humanity. The women sing in chorus and create a "music" that is "wide enough to knock the pods off chestnut trees" as Sethe stands in the doorway holding Beloved's hand. In one of the novel's most numinous images, the thirty women of the neighborhood join in song to create a sound so harmonious and powerful that it "br[eaks] the back of words." . . . Far beyond chanting, the "singing women" in this section confirm Sethe's re-instatement into the neighborhood, into motherhood, and, most importantly, into humanity. Ironically, the neighborhood women recognize their own inhuman lack of compassion in a way that the white characters of the novel never do.

Through this use of song in *Beloved*, Morrison forces the reader to identify with the humanity of her characters in the darkest era of American history, where bestiality preempts morality. Song affords the characters of her novel a form of personal testimony against the horrors of their past, and it strengthens them for the difficulties they come to accept as their future. Throughout the novel, Morrison shows how song not only has the power to "break the back" of words, but how it also destroys the numbers that the Schoolteachers of the world calculate so inhumanely. Just as the slaves' "savagery" assures Schoolteacher's "civilization," *Beloved*'s victims use song to reclaim and affirm their personhood in an aggressively inhuman world. Each time Baby Suggs adjures Sethe to "lay down [her] sword," Morrison reveals how the characters pick up a song and use it as a shield to defend and affirm their humanity. Much as Sethe "talk[s] about love with a handsaw," Toni Morrison's *Beloved* speaks to its readers about humanity with a song.

Racial Solidarity Is the Only Solution to Slavery and Racism

Doreatha Drummond Mbalia

Doreatha Drummond Mbalia is an associate professor in the Department of Africology at the University of Wisconsin, Milwaukee.

In Beloved, *Toni Morrison presents a solution to the problems of class and racial oppression she had developed in her earlier works, explains Mbalia in the following excerpt. The characters in* Beloved *who persevere are those who exhibit social responsibility and concern for each other, she states. Capitalism is the enemy facing African people today, Mbalia contends, and this enemy will be vanquished only through collaborative efforts.*

One people, one struggle one solution—this is the theme of Toni Morrison's fifth novel, *Beloved*. In her four earlier works—*The Bluest Eye, Sula, Song of Solomon,* and *Tar Baby*—Morrison demonstrates a keen awareness of, concern for, and dedication to African people. Like a scientist, she uses each work as a laboratory in which to research a hypothesis as to the nature of the oppression experienced by African people and to posit a solution to it. Starting with the issue of race as our most visible form of oppression (*The Bluest Eye*), next demonstrating that a person alone is only half a person (*Sula*), adding the problem of class exploitation to that of race (*Song of Solomon*), and then refining that idea in recognition of capitalism/imperialism as the primary target against which we

Doreatha Drummond Mbalia, *Toni Morrison's Developing Class Consciousness.* 2nd edition. Plainsboro, NJ: Susquehanna University Press, 2004. Reproduced by permission.

must struggle (*Tar Baby*), Toni Morrison uses *Beloved* as a vehicle in which to propose solidarity as the only viable solution possible for African people.

Solidarity Is the Solution

The ambivalent, uncommittal endings of the first four novels and the clear, confident ending of *Beloved* can be used as examples to gauge the author's own developing consciousness in regard to both the nature of the African's oppression and the solution. . . .

Just as *Song of Solomon*, in theme and in structure, represents a dialectical change, indeed a categorical conversion, in Toni Morrison's consciousness of herself as a part of the oppressed nation of African people, *Beloved* marks another leap in Morrison's consciousness. It is her goal in this work to demonstrate to her reader (always an African audience) that collectivism is only the first step in eradicating the national oppression and class exploitation of African people. Although never primary until this work, the intrinsic value of collectivism to the African community has always been a part of the Morrisonian canon. . . .

Just as crucial, the suicidal or homicidal nature of those Africans who divorce themselves from other Africans has also been a recurring theme. . . .

To show them the historical truth that collective struggle is the only practical solution for African people, Morrison writes a historical novel, one that explores the most oppressed period in the history of African people: slavery. By doing so, she demonstrates her clear understanding that conditions that existed then are not significantly different from those which confront African people today. That is, because Africans are faced with circumstances equally oppressive or genocidal as those in slavery, Toni Morrison shows them the life-saving benefits of uniting as one to confront a common enemy, the same enemy they struggled against more than one hundred years ago: an embryo form of capitalism. Certainly she has come to understand that [in the words of Ghanaian leader Kwame Nkrumah,] "capitalism is but the gentleman's form of slavery." Stated differently, the message conveyed in *Beloved* is as follows: No longer should African people be physically intimidated by Europeans as in *The Bluest Eye*; no longer should African people indulge in the selfish individualism of *Sula*; no longer should African people ignore their duty to pass on the knowledge of their history as in *Song of Solomon*; and no longer should African people attempt to wage struggle alone and, thus, unsuccessfully as in *Tar Baby*. Solidarity, the theme of *Beloved*, is the solution for African people.

As in previous works, Morrison's thematic astuteness is reflected in her narrative structure. In *Beloved*, on the one hand, she creates a text unencumbered by symbols indicating divisions and defiant of the linear tradition of the Western world in order to create in form what she does in substance: the qualitatively unchanged status of African people. On the other hand, she creates such a text in order to point to our solution: collectivism.

To crystallize the dire necessity of collective action to the survival of African people, Morrison juxtaposes isolated struggle with collective struggle and selfish individualism with individualism conditioned by social responsibility. In *Beloved*, most forms of isolation are genocidal for the race. Denver's isolation in life, 124's isolation in the community, and Beloved's isolation in death all serve to further divide the African community and, as a consequence, leave it vulnerable to the exploitation and oppression of the slave society. . . .

The stress on shared relationships, community, and race responsibility—the traditional African principle of collectivism—is the dominant theme of the novel. In *Beloved* life is hell, but togetherness, shared experience, and brotherly/sisterly love help the characters to survive, if not to forge better lives for themselves. This emphasis on social responsibility, the unselfish devotion of Africans helping other Africans, makes *Beloved* Toni Morrison's most conscious novel to date. . . .

Africans Economically Exploited

Crucial in her exploration of the collective solution to the African's oppression is the slave setting, for it serves to enhance the theme of *Beloved* by pointing up the dialectical relationship between problem and solution: that the solution to the problem arises from the condition (or conditions) that creates it. Simultaneously, Morrison's setting had to be one in which the strategy for solving the problem was not only clearly evident but also inevitable. For she understands that the solution then is the solution now. The most skilled method of unveiling this truth is by choosing a historical period in which the African's primary enemy, the slave system (i.e., an early form of capitalism), is unobscured by its secondary and consequential effects: race and gender oppression. In *Beloved*, gender oppression is not a visible problem that exists between African men and women, but it is one that exists within the context of the economic relationship between master and slave, and race is only a later justification for the oppression of African people. Clearly, then, Morrison's choice of setting is germane in crystallizing the nature of the African's oppression, for the economic source of both race and gender oppression is unobscured in slavery. . . .

Like gender oppression, race oppression is examined as a consequence of the economic exploitation of African people. The thesis of [historian and first prime minister of Trinidad and Tobago] Eric Williams's *Capitalism and Slavery* is threefold: that the economic demands of the budding capitalist nations led to the slave trade and slavery; that the African was enslaved primarily as a consequence of this demand (i.e., because he was a good agricultural worker, not because he was an African); and that out of the need to justify the enslavement of human beings, these nations institutionalized racism.

According to him, "Slavery was not born of racism: rather, racism was the consequence of slavery." Toni Morrison seems in agreement with Williams's thesis, for *Beloved*—while revealing that today African people are oppressed equally because of the color of their skin and their poverty—clearly proves that race was a later justification for the enslavement of African people.

To accomplish her goal of clarifying the dialectical relationship between race oppression and class exploitation, Morrison—as do Williams and others—documents history by showing that the European and the Native American Indian were enslaved before the African. . . .

The primary enemy of all three groups—the exploited European indentured servant, the Native American Indian, and the African—was and is capitalism. First the theft of raw materials for developing industrial countries and then the theft of a labor force to work within these countries gave birth to notions of inferiority and superiority that would lead to race and gender oppression. . . .

Life as a Slave Was Never Good

Of course, Morrison is most interested in documenting the history of the African in slavery. And in so doing she is at her best. Slavery, and its aftermath, come to life for the reader. First, all the history that the reader has learned about slavery is sketched out on a giant canvas: the separation of women and children from men; the treatment of slaves—both male and female, children and adults—as beasts of burden; the sexual exploitation of African women by European men. Like horses, Paul D and others like him are hitched to wagons with "bits" in their mouths. Like a cow, Sethe is milked by her slavemasters. Women, children, and men are whipped mercilessly. Stamp Paid's wife and Ella become the sexual playthings of the slavemaster. Perhaps the most vicious and cruel of all these acts was the dispersal of the race:

Black Panthers stand in formation at a rally in Oakland, California, on December 20, 1969. African American racial solidarity and self-reliance were at the core of the Black Panther Party's activism. © Bettmann/Corbis.

The last of her [Baby Suggs's] children ... she had barely glanced at when he was born because it wasn't worth the trouble to learn features you would never see change into adulthood anyway. Seven times she had done that: held a little foot, examined the fat fingertips with her own—fingers she never saw become the male or female hands a mother would recognize anywhere.

And perhaps more important than her skillful way of bringing to life the facts about slavery is Morrison's adeptness at correcting myths about slavery, the foremost of which is that slave life for some was good. Slavery was slavery, on Sweet Home as well as any other plantation. Baby Suggs testifies to this truism when Mr. Garner takes her to the European abolitionists, the Bodwins, after she is bought out of slavery by her son Halle. Mr. Garner's attempts to distinguish himself from the collective of slaveholders is regarded as a hypocritical distinction:

"Tell em, Jenny [Baby Suggs]. You live any better on any place before mine?"

"No, sir," she said. "No place. . . ."

"Ever go hungry?"

"No, sir. . . ."

"Did I let Halle buy you or not?"

"Yes, sir, you did," she said, thinking, But you got my boy and I'm all broke down. You be renting him out to pay for me way after I'm gone to Glory.

Not only were conditions in slavery qualitatively indistinguishable no matter whether you had a "good" master or a "bad" master, but also, in or out of slavery, Baby Suggs reveals that life for her has been one continuous cycle of oppression: "Her past had been like her present—intolerable." For a "free" African living in a slave society, life is not qualitatively different either.

In fact, it is to Morrison's credit that she wants the reader to make no such distinction between slavery, its aftermath, and now. . . .

With the qualitatively unchanged status of the African, Paul D's cry of desperation and frustration echoes into the present: "How much is a nigger supposed to take? Tell me. How much?" Although Stamp Paid's answer of "all he can" seems pitifully weak in light of the devastating conditions that threaten the survival of a nation of people, it is strengthened by the solution presented in this novel: solidarity. That is, Morrison demonstrates that the African's plight is less harsh and potentially extirpated if it is seen as a collective struggle: "Days of company: knowing the names of forty, fifty other Negroes, their views, habits; where they had been and what done; of feeling their fun and sorrow along with her own, . . . at 124 and in the Clearing, along with the others, she [Sethe] had claimed herself."

Unity: this is the only way African people can survive. It is only when the African, through self or forced isolation, exists outside of the collective that the struggle appears endless and the burden, unbearable. When Baby Suggs (in trying to do all the work of providing for the community by herself) and Sethe (in "trying to do it all alone with her nose in the air") and Africans in general are "resigned to life without aunts, cousins, children"—these are the times when the African's plight is intolerable. . . .

The Enemy Is Capitalism

After five novels, Toni Morrison comes to terms with both the dilemma confronting African people and a part of the solution that must be embraced by them. The novels make clear the facts that African people suffer from a crisis of the African personality, stemming from our nation-class oppression, that our primary enemy is capitalism in all of its forms and disguises, and that the solution to this crisis lies in collective, not individual, struggle against this enemy. Furthermore, Morrison crystallizes the strategy—political education through communication—which ushers in the solution: collective struggle. For it is the lack of communication that causes the major disasters in the novel: the African community does not warn Baby Suggs and Sethe of the slave trappers' approach ("Not Ella, not John, not anybody ran down or to Bluestone road, to say some new whitefolks with the Look just rode in"); Sethe does not tell Denver the reason for her murder of Beloved ("All the time, I'm afraid the thing that happened that made it all right for my [Denver's] mother to kill my sister could happen again"); and neither does Sethe ask the community for help once she is released from jail ("She returned their disapproval with the potent pride of the mistreated"). Communication—the sharing of ideas through the Word—creates the unity in the novel: the songs, gestures, and signs of slaves, the word from Hi Man as well as Baby Suggs's speaking of the

Word. It is as if Morrison is advising African people to speak the *Word* of their common history, their common plight, their common struggle, their common destiny. And she matches her theory with practice because it is through her *Word* that Africans become a more conscious people. So with the words of Stamp Paid all African people say to her: "Listen here, girl, you can't quit the Word. It's given to you to speak. You can't quit the Word." *A luta continua.* The struggle continues.

The Character Beloved Depicts the Loss of Cultural Identity That Occurred During Slavery

Lisa Williams

Lisa Williams is a professor, poet, essayist, and literary critic who teaches writing and literature at Ramapo College of New Jersey.

In Beloved *Toni Morrison explores the ways in which slavery damaged black people, not only while it was occurring, but into the present, suggests Williams in the following viewpoint. The character Beloved is used to symbolize the suffering that occurred during the passage from Africa to America as well as the suffering under slavery, Williams writes. Not only did the institution of slavery physically harm blacks, she states, but it also extinguished their language, culture, and racial identity.*

In a 1988 interview with Marsha Darling, Toni Morrison states that the character Beloved represents Sethe's murdered child as well as the collective grief of the Middle Passage. Beloved is a ghost, a child returned from the dead, and yet she is also, as Morrison says, "another kind of dead which is not spiritual but flesh, which is a survivor from the true, factual slave ship. She speaks the language, a traumatized language, of her own experience, which blends beautifully in her questions and answers, her pre-occupations, with the desires of Denver and Sethe." Sethe's personal loss is tied to the loss of those who died on the slave ship since, as Morrison says, "the language of both experiences, death and the Middle Passage—is the same."

Lisa Williams, *The Artist as Outsider in the Novels of Toni Morrison and Virginia Woolf.* Santa Barbara, CA: Greenwood Press, 2000. Reproduced with permission of ABC-CLIO, LLC, Santa Barbara, CA.

The Voice of Historical Loss

The "traumatized language" Beloved speaks, blending beautifully with the desires of Denver and Sethe, becomes the voice of historical loss that has been severed brutally from both mother and country. Beloved is the dead girl Morrison describes in a conversation with [writer] Gloria Naylor, the forgotten and silenced black girl Morrison will bring back to life through language. At the same time, she encompasses all those unrecorded people who died en route to America. Morrison explains:

> The gap between Africa and Afro-America and the gap between the living and the dead and the gap between the past and the present does not exist. It's bridged for us by our assuming responsibility for people no one's ever assumed responsibility for. They are those that died en route. Nobody knows their names, and nobody thinks about them. In addition to that, they never survived the lore; there are no songs or dances or tales of these people. The people who arrived—there is lore about them. But nothing survives about . . . that.

By creating a character that is a ghost, Morrison incorporates into her novel African beliefs in the continuing presence of the dead. Beloved represents the unvoiced horrors that took place on the slave ship. She emerges from water; her fragmented language that finds form in poetry and monologue comes from the voices of the drowned. . . . While Beloved is the vengeful child returned from the dead seeking mother love, Sethe becomes both mother and daughter in the act of killing Beloved, since she was the only surviving child; the rest were thrown overboard by her mother. As a small girl, Sethe had been told by Nan, the woman who cared for her: "She threw them all away but you. The one from the crew she threw on the island. The others from more whites she also threw away. Without names, she threw them." Sethe's mother remained nameless also, identified only by the mark on her rib, "a circle and a cross burnt right in the skin." Although Sethe was instructed by her mother to know this mark in case anything ever happened to her, at the time of her hanging, she was indistinguishable from the pile of slaves who had died and lay together. In killing Beloved, Sethe is the daughter who blends with her own mother, as she too chooses to murder her children rather than have them undergo the horrors of slavery.

Morrison acknowledges in the Darling interview that the act of dwelling on the atrocities of the Middle Passage could destroy someone and make it impossible to move forward in life. The unspoken grief of the past would obliterate both the present and the future. She says, "The act of writing the book, in a way, is a way of confronting it and making it possible to remember." Morrison gives voice to those thrown overboard without names, as well as those nameless bodies burnt and marked by slavery.

The Past Is Always Present

As in her previous novels, Morrison narrates what has been left out of language; she accomplishes this by structuring the novel so that history and memory are what define the present moment. "Rememory," as Sethe describes it, is the process by which memory becomes a repetitive act. The past enters the present moment in fragments, so that history is ever present in the consciousness of Morrison's characters, even if it is absorbed by the mind frame by frame, in scenes and pictures that come clearly into focus through the touch of a hand, a kiss on a brutalized back, or the sight of snow falling on familiar land. . . .

Loss of Language, Culture, and Identity

Morrison is concerned, in particular, with the massive destruction of culture, of language and identity, and its effect on the present moment. If Morrison says in her Nobel Prize

Speech that words can never properly express the horrors of slavery or the 600,000 dead in the Civil War, but can only "arc toward the place where meaning may lie," then the shadow that holds hands while the people do not becomes symbolic of the necessity of using language to suggest meaning. The constraining nature of a static language is incapable of capturing the unvoiced and unrecorded grief of the dead.

Loss and mourning, and "history that will not be kept at bay," all come together in the ghost of Beloved, the fully dressed woman who "walked out of the water." . . . Beloved arises from the murkiness of water, and her wrath, which becomes directed at her mother, is simultaneously the rage of those who, despite the process of rememory, live outside of static language and the records of history. In creating Beloved, Morrison, on the other hand, uses language that is, [critic] Iain Chambers describes, "always shadowed by loss, an elsewhere, a ghost."

As a ghost, Beloved is the true migrant, the one with no home, no borders, not even between the living and the dead; and her restless and frustrated wandering evokes the pain of the unburied dead who have found no peaceful passage. . . . Beloved links African and African-American experience. As a totally displaced human being, she becomes the voice of the hybridization of African culture that occurred during slavery.

She exists in a watery realm that is neither fully dead nor alive. Her exquisite monologue is told in poetic fragments, without punctuation, as though to accent the absence of borders between the past, present and future, as well as the living and the dead. Her language evokes the homelessness and loss created by history. She gives voice to her own experience as well as the collective grief of those who died during the Middle Passage. Beloved says in her "traumatized language": "now there is room to crouch and to watch the crouching others it is the crouching that is now always now inside the woman with my face is in the sea a hot thing." . . .

Beloved speaks in a fractured language. She remembers the loss of her mother amidst the large-scale brutalities taking place:

> in the beginning the women are away from the men and the men are away from the women storms rock us and mix the men into the women and the women into the men that is when I begin to be on the back of the men for a long time I see only his neck and his wide shoulders above me I am small I love him because he has a song When he turned around to die I see the teeth he sang through his singing was soft his singing is of the place where a woman takes flowers away from their leaves and puts them in a round basket.

Beloved's prose poem moves from the horrors of a ship to the longing for her mother. She wonders: "how can I say things that are pictures I am not separate from her There is no place where I stop Her face is my own and I want to be there in the place where her face is and to be looking at it too a hot thing."

Beloved's words blend the present experience of finally finding her lost mother with the past losses associated with slavery. The very spaces between words evoke African religious belief in an eternal universe unbounded by space and time. This way of viewing the world leads naturally to a concern primarily with the past and present, since the future is expected to continue without ever ending. In fact, Beloved's words shift back and forth through time, echoing the ravages of history and the wish to be reunited with her mother.

This monologue, told from the daughter's point of view, speaks of what it is like to be ruptured from one's point of origin. . . .

Beloved's sudden arrival from the world of the dead emphasizes the belief in parts of Africa that the next world may be invisible, but exists in a realm that is very close to the living with its own share of lakes, forests, mountains and animals that can be seen only by the dead. Rigid divisions do not exist between the earth and the places where the dead dwell. Moreover, improperly buried and mourned for, torn from her mother and the country of her ancestors, Beloved's extreme thirst and overwhelming fatigue upon her arrival at 124 suggest the long length of time she has spent in search of her home.

Community Has the Power to Heal

In this novel, Morrison portrays the grief Black mothers experienced due to slavery. In fact, Toni Morrison says that her novel is about "among other things, the tension between being yourself, one's own Beloved, and being a mother." While Sethe may have been able to escape from slavery, she could not escape from the strangling confines of motherhood. . . .

For Sethe, the robbing of her milk, an act that is a direct attack on her as a Black mother, only makes her cling more strongly to her children. The realities of slavery and the isolation she experiences from the community after the murder of Beloved forces her to raise her children alone. Even after Beloved's murder, she reluctantly lets Baby Suggs hold Denver. And when Sethe stops going to work because she cannot bear to leave the dead child who has returned to her, her happiness is short-lived. The glee she feels while skating on the ice with her children is soon replaced by the pain of Beloved's vengeance. Like the other carnivalesque episodes in the novel, joy turns suddenly into its opposite. Beloved's need for maternal love is rapacious, and her demand for reparation leads to Sethe's deterioration. This self-contained community of storytelling women is transformed into a household where it is now up to Denver, as the stabilizing force for both Beloved and Sethe, to save her mother.

The isolation of Sethe's mother-love gives way to the community's intervention at the end of the novel. In the last pages of *Beloved*, each character looks at the present surroundings and can only see the images of the past. The thirty women who come to Sethe's house to save her do not see Denver sitting on the steps, but themselves, "younger, stronger, even as little girls lying in the grass asleep." Even Baby Suggs arises from the dead as a testament to the ritualized and eternal nature of memory:

> Baby Suggs laughed and skipped among them, urging more. Mothers dead now moved their shoulders to mouth harps. The fence they had leaned on and climbed over was gone. The stump of the butternut had split like a fan. But there they were, young and happy, playing in Baby Suggs' yard, not feeling the envy that surfaced the next day.

The party too resurfaces again to form a major image that links the novel together. Time, like language itself, is cyclic and cannot conform to rigid definitions of chronology. As Ella hollers at the thought of Sethe's dead daughter, "coming back to whip," the sound Ella makes brings the women back into an awareness of a time that is pre-linguistic: "Instantly the kneelers and the standers joined her. They stopped praying and took a step back to the beginning. In the beginning, there were no words. In the beginning was the sound, and they all knew what that sound sounded like." . . .

As Sethe gazes at the women approaching her, she can hear the healing sounds of Baby Suggs in their voices:

> For Sethe it was as though the clearing had come to her with all its heat and simmering leaves, where the voices of women searched for the right combination, the key, the code, the sound that broke the back of words. Building voice upon voice until they found it, and when they did it was a wave of sound wide enough to sound deep water and knock the pods off chestnut trees. It broke over Sethe and she trembled like the baptized in its wash.

It is the sounds from the community of women that have the capacity to heal, to break "the back of words" used to justify violence. The women communally build a choral sound that can wash the wounds inflicted by people like Schoolteacher. But if Sethe sees Baby Suggs' congregation in the faces of the women, that image is replaced by Bodwin's black hat, an object bringing Schoolteacher back into the present. Sethe cannot distinguish the non-threatening hat of the present from the violation that hat had brought her in the past. She believes "he is coming into her yard and he is coming for her best thing." In a similar way that Baby Suggs' party from years ago blended into the arrival of Schoolteacher, this same process takes place in Sethe's memory in the present moment. She first recalls Baby Suggs and then believes Schoolteacher is back when she sees Bodwin's hat. Each time the memory is related to an object that brings the past clearly into the present. At the same time, the language of healing, of sound without words, is posited against Schoolteacher's violent acts, his brutality that is justified by his rational, linear use of sexist, racist language.

Even the incantory effect of Morrison's repeating phrase in the last pages of the novel, "it was not a story to pass on," suggests a meaning that is its very opposite. Beloved disappears once she witnesses her mother's attempt to murder Bodwin, as though the re-enactment and subsequent desire to rewrite the past leads Beloved back to the place where the dying dwell. Although Beloved may be "disremembered and unaccounted for," a footprint that comes and goes around the stream of 124, the novel finds form for her fragmented story, form for the sound beyond the silence, ultimately affirming by its very structure that this is a story that must and will be passed on.

An African American Identity Was Forged by Slavery

Timothy L. Parrish

Timothy L. Parrish is a professor of English at Southern Connecticut State University.

There are both similarities and differences in the way Toni Morrison and novelist Charles Johnson address the impact slavery has had on African Americans, Parrish explains in the following essay. According to Parrish, both writers agree that the experience of slavery shaped an African American identity and culture during slavery and into the present day. However, Johnson sees African American identity as a blending with other American cultures, while Morrison suggests that African American culture is distinctly different from white culture.

The slave narrative, as Hazel V. Carby points out [in "Ideologies of Black Folk: The Historical Novel of Slavery"], differs from the historical novel of slavery in that the prior form is concerned exclusively with how "the ex-slaves 'wrote [their selves] into being' through an account of the condition of being a slave." The contemporary writer, in contrast, can only re-imagine the conditions of slavery, and therefore writes in order to connect the receding past to the living present. This distinction underscores the difference between recalling slavery as an ex-slave versus reconstructing slavery as one who would understand how its history continues to shape one's present. Yet to say that the slave narrative focuses on how the ex-slaves wrote their selves into being is also to imply that the ex-slaves had no identity prior to writing it. While not dis-

Timothy L. Parrish, "Imagining Slavery: Toni Morrison and Charles Johnson," *Studies in American Fiction*, vol. 25, Spring 1997, p. 81. © 1997 Northeastern University. Reproduced by permission of The Johns Hopkins University Press.

agreeing with Carby's distinction, I suggest that both forms confront the question: how do I reinvent myself in light of my altered circumstance? Seen this way, the question of how one connects oneself to (or disconnects oneself from) the experience of slavery has been a preeminent concern for all African-American writers from the time of slave narratives on. . . . The barrier that one crosses over in moving from slavery to freedom is also the point at which the continuity of African-American identity is imagined and created.

Identity Forged by Slavery

Indeed, one could almost say that whereas the writers of the slave narratives were intent on inventing their free selves, contemporary African-American writers have been intent on inventing their slave selves. . . . Of the many novelists who have taken up slavery, I single out *Beloved* (1987) by Toni Morrison and *Oxherding Tale* (1982) by Charles Johnson in part because these two writers seem to be offering diametrically opposing views on the meaning of slavery, in part because I would like to suggest that Morrison and Johnson may be closer than a first reading would suggest. Both writers explore how African-American identity was forged in the crucible of slavery, and how that identity continues to be created today. Their basic difference resides in how they interpret the meaning of that ongoing cultural invention, specifically as it relates to American identity. . . . *Oxherding Tale* concludes with a happy mulatto marriage. . . . No such ending is imaginable in *Beloved* or in Morrison's fiction generally. Morrison invokes the ghost of slavery in order to illuminate the continuity of African-American identity—a community originating in the shared experience of slavery. Insofar as she brings slavery to the present day, Morrison's African-American community is at once a part of and separate from so-called white American experience. Johnson, on the other hand, imagines African-American identity to be irretrievably mixed with other American identities, a happy mongrel. For Johnson, slavery is less a historical presence than a philosophical problem. Although Johnson and Morrison offer differing views of how to view the present, each writer understands that the meaning of slavery cannot be recaptured, but only re-seen. . . .

For his part, Johnson has been eager to distinguish his work from Morrison's, declaring that *Beloved* is "not an intellectual achievement." This remark means to suggest that Morrison is philosophically less sophisticated than Johnson in her approach because, unlike him, she is trying to recover an essentialized, racialized African-American identity. Below I examine the ways in which Morrison invites this critique but ultimately, in my view, offers a reading of slavery and African-American identity more complex than Johnson would allow. The work of both Johnson and Morrison takes part in an ongoing revision—historical and literary—that emphasizes the agency of African-Americans in creating a culture not defined solely in opposition to white definitions of black selfhood. . . .

Freedom and Slavery Not Opposites

The crucial difference between Johnson and Morrison inheres in how each writer explores the barrier between slavery and freedom. Neither finally thinks that the experience of slavery, however we define it, can be known exactly for what it was. Morrison, though, is reluctant to surrender the idea that an intimate knowledge of slavery can be recovered and shared. Unlike Johnson, she positions Sethe on the painful border between slavery and freedom and leaves her there for most of the novel. As a result, Morrison's depiction of the past seems to some more beholden, less flexible than Johnson's. On the contrary, I think that what makes Morrison's *Beloved* as profound an encounter with the past as, say, [William] Faulkner's *Absalom, Absalom!* is her willingness to risk losing her characters and even her narrative voice in a past that can be neither seen nor controlled, but which nevertheless surrounds the novel's every action. . . .

Beloved is a historical novel about slavery that tries to understand the story that the slave narrative could not tell. Consider Frederick Douglass's *Narrative of the Life of An Ex-Slave* (1845). Douglass depicts slavery as a moral evil to be escaped. His story of origins portrays the triumph of his own humanity over the inhuman conditions into which he was born. Morrison's work contests in a rather shocking way the assumption of Douglass's *Narrative* that free/slave are mutually opposed terms. Sethe's story embodies the impossibility of maintaining this opposition. Thus, in the interim between escaping from Sweet Home and murdering her child, Beloved, Sethe believes that she has "claimed herself." However, this sense of self-possession disappears when her "owners" arrive to reclaim her. That terrible moment is the focal point of *Beloved* because it is when Sethe first realizes all that she has had to repress in order to survive as a slave. Reaching out to kill her family and herself is her first act of freedom. Toni Morrison identified the meaning of Sethe's gesture and staked out the aim of her novel in her remark that "the best thing that is in us is also the thing that makes us sabotage ourselves." Yet Sethe's act of murder is also an act of self-possession—an idea that Johnson explores in *The Oxherding Tale*. The problem for Morrison becomes how a necessary act of murder can be transformed into a healing act of recovery. Sethe's story dramatizes how claiming ownership of one's freed self is impossible without recovering the self that she disowned in the name of freedom—what is her own best thing. . . .

The Slave Experience Was Collective

By addressing slavery's unrepresentability as well as the paradoxical soul-killing that freedom demands, Morrison shows us that Douglass's—or any slave's—journey into freedom did not belong to one person. Understanding the slaves' journey into freedom as an essentially individual one distorts the experience of those slaves—the majority—whose journey could not

A 1917 photograph of a chain gang building a road. According to Timothy L. Parrish, Morrison portrays the shared experience of oppression as a source of African American solidarity. © Bettmann/Corbis.

have mirrored Douglass's. This "individual" story also distorts the future since it fairly obliterates the fact that the slaves' journey was a collective experience, making for a collective history and future (and present, Morrison would add). The sense of community lost and found is movingly captured in the story of Paul D's escape from the chain gang in Georgia. Technically, Paul D is no longer a slave, but the chains of slavery have become the shackles of the chain gang. For all practical purposes, his status has not changed at all. Paul D reflects that even as a prisoner (or a slave) the pleasure of listening to the doves was denied him since he had "neither the right nor the permission to enjoy it because in that place mist, doves, sunlight, copper, dirt, moon—everything belonged to the men who had the guns." Yet one thing does belong to Paul D and that is the experience he shares with the other prisoners, the feeling they share from being chained to one another, hand by hand, link by link. Together they sang it out and beat it up, garbling the words so they could

not be understood; tricking the words so their syllables

yielded up other meanings. They sang . . . of pork in the

woods, meal in the pan; fish on the line; cane, rain, and

rocking chairs.

Like Douglass's singing slaves, Morrison's singing prisoners create an identity separate from their imprisonment. This separate identity enables them to survive their imprisonment.

Though the prisoners remain chained to one another, a group, the imprisoners make sure that each prisoner is caparisoned within his own box. This creates a tension between a life-affirming communal identity and a death-dealing individual one. One night the rains pour down, filling each cubicle up with water, and there is the possibility that each man will drown—alone. Suddenly, "somebody yanked the chain," the group of prisoners moves as one, burrowing under the mud, arriving safe on the other side of their imprisoning box. "For one lost, all lost. The chain that held them would save all or none."

The source of African-American identity, Morrison tell us, derives from this shared experience of oppression. Their freedom does not issue from a white man's piece of paper; it is the result of the strength and the resolve they discovered together from within their days of bondage. . . .

A Collective Journey

In comparing Morrison and Johnson, [Molly Able Travis in "Beloved and Middle Passage: Race, Narrative and the Critic's Essentialism,"] suggests that Morrison wants "to return to the past" to discover the gaps of cultural memory while Johnson "leaves behind the notion of a memory to be recovered." . . . Unquestionably, Morrison looks to the past with a more longing eye than Johnson does, but the formulation that Morrison seeks the past while Johnson looks to the future risks refusing each writer her or his complexity. The real lesson is that the meaning of the slaves' heritage remains fluid—a kind of ongoing collective work. Hence, Morrison's characters come to terms with the realization that their community exists not in Africa, but in the collective experience of the crossing, symbolized by the mark. Likewise, *Oxherding Tale*'s Andrew Hawkins does not so much will his freedom, as Douglass did, but is free only insofar as he understands himself to be an ongoing revision of his past. More than one hundred and twenty-five years after slavery ended, African Americans continue to write their selves into being. In this respect, Andrew makes a remark that I think Morrison would find compelling: "memory, as the metaphysicians say, is imagination." In *Beloved* and *Oxherding Tale*, Morrison and Johnson reimagine the journey that African Americans continue to make in order to arrive in the present.

Slavery Robbed African Americans of Their Personal Identities

Jennifer L. Holden

Jennifer L. Holden has been a lecturer at the University of California–Riverside.

Slavery turned human beings into objects and denied them their freedom and humanity, Holden contends in the following viewpoint. According to Holden, the characters in Beloved *are haunted by the experience of slavery, and even though they have been legally freed, they struggle to attain personal subjectivity, or freedom. With support from the community, Denver is finally able to assert her freedom, the author asserts.*

In a 1989 interview with Bonnie Angelo of *Time* magazine, Toni Morrison discussed the desire of our nation to repress the memory of slavery. According to Morrison, the enslavement of Africans and African Americans in the United States is "something that the characters [in *Beloved*] don't want to remember, I don't want to remember, black people don't want to remember, white people don't want to remember." Yet her novel forces its reader to recognize the existence and conditions of slavery in a nation that would prefer to forget that such a crime was ever committed. While Morrison, like Sethe and Paul D., would prefer to repress the memory of slavery, she feels compelled to create a space in which the "enslaved" may finally speak. . . .

While the end of slavery sought to transform objects (slaves) into subjects (free men and women), the characters in

Jennifer L. Holden, "Looking into the Self That Is No Self: An Examination of Subjectivity in Beloved," *African American Review*, vol. 23, Fall 1998, p. 415. Reproduced by permission of the author.

Beloved find the passage into subjectivity somewhat elusive. In this essay, I explore the question of Beloved's identity and how her identity affects her own subjectivity, as well as that of Denver and Sethe. First, I explain how Beloved's perpetual references to a slave ship experience function as her primal scene: [which Sigmund Freud defined as] a traumatic event in one's childhood which may be considered the cause of one's adult neurosis. After interpreting the primal scene, I discuss the complexity of Beloved's identity. As Margaret Atwood asserts, "There's a lot more to Beloved than any one character can see, and she manages to be many things to several people." Like the novel itself, the character of Beloved resists a singular interpretation. However, if for a moment one were to disregard the multiplicity of Beloved's voice and focus instead on the voice as a single consciousness, one would find a powerful way into the novel. This schema allows the reader to consider another possible interpretation of Beloved's identity. Finally, I examine the characters' desire for subjectivity and the extent to which their desires are fulfilled.

Identifying the Primal Scene

In her article "Toni Morrison's Ghost: The Beloved Who Is Not Beloved," Elizabeth B. House informs us that "unraveling the mystery of . . . [Beloved's] identity depends to a great extent upon first deciphering chapters four and five of Part II" in *Beloved*. House provides a detailed explanation of the obscure references in the narrative, pointing out "how white slave traders . . . captured the girl and her mother" and "put them aboard an abysmally crowded slave ship." . . .

In *Black Cargo*, Richard Howard illustrates the condition and treatment of African men, women, and children aboard a typical slave ship. Quoting Harry Johnston, he tells how the kidnapped people were kept

> "enclosed under grated hatchways, between deck. The space was so low that they sat between each other's legs, and

stowed so close together that there was no possibility of lying down, or at all changing their positions by night or day.
As they belonged to, and were shipped on account of different individuals, they were all branded like sheep . . . burnt
with a red-hot iron."

With this account in mind, the reader can recognize what
Morrison is referring to with phrases like "I am always crouching," "someone is thrashing but there is no room to do it in,"
and especially the repeated "a hot thing." Once the sequence
has been recognized as an experience from the Middle Passage, the reader is able to translate previously ambiguous references. The "men without skin" are clearly white sailors who
offer their urine ("morning water") and moldy ("sea-colored")
bread to the dehydrated Africans. The "little hill," a pile of
dead bodies, is pushed from the bridge of the ship into the
ocean. Later, it appears as if one of the white sailors or officers
takes the young girl "inside" a cabin and rapes her: "I am going to be in pieces," she says, "he hurts where I sleep he puts
his finger there I drop the food and break into pieces." These
and other allusions to the treatment and condition of Africans
during the Middle Passage emerge in the narrative of *Beloved*.

The nineteen- or twenty-year-old woman who arrives at
Sethe's house possesses the subjectivity of the African girl held
captive on the slave ship in Part II. Nearly every reference the
young woman makes, or question that she asks, derives from
either her experience in Africa before being captured or her
experience on the slave ship during the Middle Passage. The
intensity of her memory indicates that the events of and sur-
rounding the slave ship represent her primal scene. . . .

Beloved's references to the primal scene continue to arise
and be interpreted in various ways by the other characters
throughout the novel. When Beloved asks Sethe, "'Where your
diamonds?'" Sethe assumes that she is asking about Mrs.
Garner's crystal earrings. However, Beloved may be seeking
her mother's "shining," "sharp earrings" that the "men without

skin" stole on the slave ship. When Denver accuses Beloved of choking Sethe in the Clearing, Beloved innocently replies, "'I kissed her neck. I didn't choke it. The circle of iron choked it.'" In the primal scene, Beloved views the "circle around her [mother's] neck" and wishes that she could "bite" it off. On another occasion, Beloved is humming an African song, which is most likely the tune she hears through the teeth of "the dying man" on the ship: "his singing was soft . . . of the place where a woman takes flowers away from their leaves and puts them in a round basket." When Beloved explains how she "got on the bridge" and searched for her mother's face, Denver assumes that she is referring to a bridge in the woods. However, Beloved is most likely referring to the bridge of the slave ship.

Near the end of the novel, Beloved becomes almost solely preoccupied with the primal scene: "Sometimes she screamed, 'Rain! Rain!' and clawed her throat. . . . Other times Beloved curled up on the floor, her wrists between her knees, and stayed there for hours . . . She would go to Sethe, run her fingers over the woman's teeth while tears slid from her wide black eyes." When Beloved cries out "'Rain!'" she appears to be remembering "standing in the rain falling . . . falling like the rain is," while observing the death of her mother from the ship's bridge. In curling up on the floor, Beloved seems to be illustrating the incessant "crouching" in the hull of the slave ship. Running her fingers over Sethe's teeth and crying, Beloved seems to be envisioning the "pretty little teeth" of the dead man on her face and mourning his absence.

When the primal scene leaves the realm of hallucination for Beloved and appears to repeat itself in the historical present, Beloved suddenly vanishes. As she sees Sethe "running away from her" and "feels the emptiness in [her] hand," Beloved knows that she is being left "alone. Again." The scene directly parallels Beloved's loss of her African mother on the slave ship. Standing on the ship's bridge, Beloved helplessly watches as the slave traders amass a pile of dead bodies and push them into the sea. Beloved's horror is intensified when she discovers that her mother has willfully joined the mound of people: "the men without skin . . . push my own man through they do not push her she goes in the little hill is gone." Her mother's suicide causes Beloved to feel abandoned and betrayed. As Beloved stands on the porch of 124, she once again experiences the abandonment of her mother (whom she considers Sethe to be): ". . . she is running into the faces of the people out there, joining them and leaving Beloved behind. . . . They make a hill. A hill of black people, falling."

The imagined re-enactment of her mother's suicide and the ensuing feelings of loss, emptiness, and betrayal overwhelm Beloved to such an extent that she instantaneously disappears. When Freud and one of his patients uncovered the primal scene, where the patient's disorder originated, the discovery enabled the patient to overcome his or her illness. By encouraging the patient to confront his/her primal scene instead of turning away from it, Freud believed that the recovery process was expedited. Beloved does not retract from previous encounters with her primal scene, since in those instances she is able to control the memory. In the final scene, however, Beloved is confronted with the traumatic experience and possesses no control over what is happening. It is at this moment of loss of all control that Beloved flees the primal scene.

Unraveling Beloved's Identity

Since the publication of Morrison's novel in 1987, the identity of Beloved has perplexed some readers, annoyed others, and intrigued the majority. Most readers and critics share Thomas R. Edwards's perspective that Beloved "is unquestionably the dead daughter's spirit in human form." However, Walter Clemons argues that, since the murdered baby could not have remembered passage on a slave ship, "Beloved is also a ghost from the slave ships of Sethe's ancestry." Deborah Horvitz expands upon Clemons's assertion, concluding that Beloved "is

A 1930s lithograph by Bernarda Bryson Shahn depicting a slave ship. Jennifer L. Holden discusses the references to the Middle Passage and the slave ship experience in Morrison's novel Beloved. © Corbis.

not only Sethe's two-year-old daughter, whom she murdered eighteen years ago; she is also Sethe's African mother." House contradicts all prior critics by contending that Beloved "is not a supernatural being of any kind but simply a young woman who has herself suffered the horrors of slavery." The many interpretations of Beloved's identity reveal the complexity of Morrison's character. Not only is she read differently by different characters in the novel but also by different readers of the novel. Each new interpretation of Beloved adds another layer to her already thick identity.

My reading of Beloved differs from the interpretations cited above. Since the child that Sethe murders is born in America and never travels the Middle Passage, the proposal that Beloved is solely the reincarnated baby seems highly unlikely, if not impossible. . . .

I will argue that the African girl in the Middle Passage sequence is Sethe's mother before she reaches America and gives birth to Sethe, the only baby she did not throw away.

"Of that place where she was born (Carolina maybe? or was it Louisiana?)" Sethe remembers singing and dancing, but close to nothing about her mother. Upon Beloved's arrival, however, Sethe's repressed memories of her mother slowly begin to re-emerge. When Sethe sees the young woman's face for the first time, she has an uncontrollable need to urinate. Sethe recalls having not "had an emergency that unmanageable . . . since she was a baby girl, being cared for by the eight-year-old girl who pointed out her mother to her." Sethe's reaction of the appearance of Beloved may be viewed in Freudian terms as "'das Unheimliche'": an uncanny experience which "is in reality nothing new or alien, but something which is familiar and old-established in the mind and which has become alienated from it only through the process of repression." The sight of Beloved causes Sethe to reenact a childhood experience—one that she specifically relates to her mother. In his essay entitled "The 'Uncanny,'" Freud reveals how the source of uncanny feelings in an adult may be either an "infantile fear" or "an infantile wish or even merely an infantile belief." Since Beloved's uncanniness arouses neither fear nor particular pleasure in Sethe, one may view the uncanny feeling as mere recognition of a repressed figure from her childhood. While Sethe initially makes the connection between the present and the past experience, she later attributes her weak bladder to a subconscious recognition of her dead daughter, eliding all possible connections of Beloved to her mother.

Sethe reveals more details about her mother as the novel progresses. In one instance, Sethe recalls Nan telling her that she and Sethe's mother "were together from the sea" and "taken up many times by the crew." Nan and Sethe's mother were on the same slave ship during the Middle Passage and were both raped by white sailors. Their experiences aboard the vessel parallel the experience that Beloved relates in section II. The "language" that Nan and Sethe's mother spoke differs from the language Sethe uses now. The pronunciation of her mother's words also differs, as illustrated and emphasized when her Ma'am calls her "Seth - thuh" instead of "Sethe." Beloved's "gravelly voice . . . with a cadence not like" Sethe's or Denver's and her peculiar expressions, like "my woman" instead of "mother," parallel Sethe's memory of her mother's unfamiliar language and unusual accent. Of course, the language and accent that pervade Beloved's and Sethe's mother's speech are residually African.

The "song and dance" that Sethe remembers from her childhood also originate in Africa. In particular, Sethe recalls how

> . . . sometimes they danced the antelope. The men as well as the ma'ams, one of whom was certainly her own. They shifted shapes and became something other. Some unchained, demanding others whose feet knew her pulse better than she did.

When dancing for Denver, Beloved does "a little two-step, two-step, make-a-new-step, slide, slide and strut on down." Although her dance is untitled, it is possible that Beloved's movements emulate some kind of African dance. The exhilaration that Sethe recalls seeing in the men and women who danced the "antelope" is mirrored in Beloved's dance, as she and Denver move "round and round the tiny room," swinging "to and fro, to and fro, until exhausted."

The "song" that Sethe claims to have invented to sing to her children appears to be of partly African origin as well. When Beloved begins humming a particular melody, Sethe assumes that the young woman is her dead child, since she is confident that "nobody knows that song but me and my children." Beloved does not sing any of the song's lyrics; she only hums the song's tune. As an adult, Sethe made up the words to the song, but the melody of the song most likely derives from the place "before Sweet Home." Since she "could neither recall nor repeat" the language spoken in that place, it would be impossible for Sethe to recreate the words to any African songs. However, the melody of a specific song may very well have been subconsciously retained and revived later on in her adult life. As pointed out earlier, the origin of the song for Beloved is on the slave ship, where she listens to the "song" of the man who lies above her. Apparently, the melody that Beloved hears in the Middle Passage and recites in Sethe's home is the same melody that Sethe hears as a child while in the presence of her mother and/or her mother's people.

In describing her mother's appearance, Sethe remarks that "she'd had the bit so many times she smiled. When she wasn't smiling she smiled, and I never saw her own smile." Beloved is frequently described as wearing a perpetual smile. When she emerges from the stream, she is described as an unusual sight, causing people who may have seen her to hesitate "before approaching her. Not because she was wet, or dozing or had what sounded like asthma, but because amid all that she was smiling." When the thirty singing women assemble in Sethe's front yard to chase away the "devil-child," Beloved remains standing on the porch "naked and smiling." Even after Sethe races across the yard to attack Edward Bodwin, leaving Beloved "alone," she continues to smile. People had informed Sethe that "it was the bit that made her [mother] smile when she didn't want to." While Beloved shows no physical indications of ever having worn a bit, she occasionally illustrates the uncontrollable smile of a woman who has.

The strongest piece of evidence identifying Beloved as Sethe's mother can be observed in the final chapter of the novel. "When once or twice Sethe tried to assert herself—be the unquestioned mother whose word was law and who knew what was best—Beloved slammed things," rejecting Sethe's role as mother. Eventually, Sethe relinquishes her position as Beloved's mother altogether and falls into the position of Beloved's daughter:

Beloved bending over Sethe looked the mother, Sethe the teething child, for other than those times when Beloved needed her, Sethe confined herself to a corner chair. The bigger Beloved got, the smaller Sethe became. . . .

This reversal of roles seems to function as the unveiling of an alternate identity for each woman, even though none of the characters in the novel seem to recognize the significance of the transformation. . . .

Searching for Subjectivity

When Beloved accuses Sethe of "leaving her behind. Of not being nice to her, not smiling at her," she seems to be referring to her mother, who left her behind on the slave ship. Sethe responds by "saying she had to get them out, away, that she had the milk all the time . . . [t]hat her plan was always that they would all be together on the other side, forever." Sethe hears what she expects her daughter would say and fails to comprehend the details of Beloved's accusations; Sethe assumes that Beloved's descriptions of starvation, rape, "dead men," and "ghosts without skin" apply to hell, purgatory, or some form of afterlife beyond Sethe's understanding and control. When Sethe relates to Beloved how she took care of her as a baby, Beloved denies her devotion. No matter what Sethe says, Beloved sits in a chair, "uncomprehending everything except that Sethe was the woman who took her face away, leaving her crouching in a dark, dark place, forgetting to smile." The scene is tragic, as Sethe pleads for forgiveness from a woman who may not be her child, and Beloved begs for an explanation from a woman who may not be her mother. Each woman's desire can be read as a demand for recognition from the other. According to Barbara Shapiro, "The craving for mutual recognition—for simultaneously 'seeing' the beloved other and being 'seen' by her—propels the central characters in the novel." Sethe and Beloved need to be recognized by the other in order to become subjects of the symbolic order. . . .

Because Beloved appears to consider Sethe her mother from the Middle Passage, Sethe's gaze is the only one that can restore Beloved's identity. In the slave ship sequence, Beloved believes that she and her mother share a single identity: "I am not separate from her there is no place where I stop." The young girl engages in transitivism, viewing her mother as a mere extension of herself rather than as a separate subject. When the man above her "locks his eyes and dies on [her] face," she says that she is able to see her mother. However, what Beloved probably sees is her own face in the reflection of the dead man's glassed-over eyes. Beloved's loss of identity occurs when her mother "goes in" the sea. Since she is unable to distinguish between her mother's face and her own, Beloved's identity is cast into the water along with her mother's body. Without her mother, she has no "name," no "face," and "no one to want" her. When Beloved sees Sethe's face, she believes that Sethe's "is the one. She is the one I need."

Sethe's mother Beloved comes back from the dead hoping to receive the attention, affection, and recognition from her mother that she had lost when her mother committed suicide on the slave ship. . . .

Because Beloved is not recognized as Sethe's mother, her need to establish her identity and regain her subjectivity remains unfulfilled. "Although she has claim, she is not claimed," and without being "claimed," Beloved "erupts into her separate parts, to make it easy for the chewing laughter to swallow her all away."

For Sethe, Beloved's disappearance means the dissolution of her own subjectivity. When Paul D. finally resolves to see her, he finds her in Baby Suggs's bed apparently awaiting her death. He tells Sethe of his intention to bathe and massage her feet, and she thinks to herself: "There's nothing to rub now and no reason to. Nothing left to bathe, assuming he even knows how." Without Beloved, Sethe believes that her body, like her self no longer exists. Only Paul D. can begin to convince her that she has access to subjectivity outside of the maternal, as he insists, "'You your best thing, Sethe. You are.'" Sethe's closing response, "'Me? Me?'" seems to imply that she may in time come to recognize and claim her own subjectivity.

While Beloved never attains subjectivity and Sethe only approaches it, Denver firmly asserts her subjectivity at the end of the novel. Denver knew that the only way to protect her mother from Beloved was "to leave the yard; step off the edge of the world, leave the two behind and go ask somebody for help." However, she cannot find the strength to leave 124 without the encouragement of her deceased grandmother. Baby Suggs had once told Denver that "there was no defense" against white people. Now, she instructs her granddaughter to "'know it, and go on out the yard. Go on.'" Realizing that not only Sethe's but her own well-being depended on her finding a job, Denver begins to regard herself as having a self: "It was a new thought, having a self to look out for and preserve." She soon begins to work nights for the Bodwins and seeks a day job in a shirt factory as well. Denver's assertion of subjectivity is accentuated when Paul D. offers her his opinion on Beloved and she abruptly declines, saying, "'I have my own'" opinion. She acknowledges her own self and requires neither the look of her mother nor Beloved to attain subjectivity.

Through *Beloved*, Morrison reveals how slavery and the period of Reconstruction failed to grant subjectivity to many African Americans. Those who did gain subjectivity did so by their own assertion, as American society was reluctant legally and socially to acknowledge African Americans as valid citizens. For the characters in the novel, the transition from object to subject presents many obstacles; however, with the support and encouragement from voices of the past (Baby Suggs for Denver, Paul D. for Sethe), subjectivity becomes attainable.

Beloved Exposes the Psychological Trauma Caused by Slavery

J. Brooks Bouson

Author and literary critic J. Brooks Bouson is a professor of English at Loyola University Chicago.

A white supremacist society traumatized blacks through physical and psychological abuse, Bouson claims in the following viewpoint. Whites perceived blacks to be no different from animals, Bouson states. Humiliated, abused, and shamed by their white oppressors, blacks developed feelings of inferiority.

Continuing the cultural and literary labor of her earlier novels in *Beloved*, Morrison shows just how much race has mattered historically to African Americans as she explores the cultural "roots" of black Americans in slavery. As Morrison examines the white supremacist ideology and essentialist discursive repertoires that defined the African-American slave as the racial Other—as biologically inferior, morally degenerate, and animalistic—she focuses attention on the formative and "dirtying" power of racist representations. She also dramatizes the social and political consequences of racist thinking and practices in *Beloved*, describing not only the humiliations and traumas the slaves were forced to endure at the hands of their white oppressors but also the insidious effects of internalized racism—that is, socially produced feelings of self-contempt and self-hatred—on the construction of African-American identities. . . .

J. Brooks Bouson, *Quiet as It's Kept: Shame, Trauma, and Race in the Novels of Toni Morrison*. Albany: State University of New York Press, 2000. © 2000, State University of New York. All rights reserved. Reproduced by permission of the State University of New York Press.

The Damage Done by White Supremacy

Through the portrayal of her slave mother character, Sethe, Morrison attempts to expose a truth about the interior life of the historical figure, Margaret Garner. A slave who escaped from Kentucky to Cincinnati, Ohio, Margaret Garner attempted to kill all four of her children when her slave owner found her, and she actually succeeded in killing one child, an infant daughter. Morrison has commented that she deliberately avoided doing extensive research on the Margaret Garner case—a case she first became interested in while editing *The Black Book*, which was published in 1974—because she "wanted to invent" Margaret Garner's life and "be accessible to anything the characters had to say about it." "[W]hat struck me," Morrison recalls, was that when Margaret Garner was interviewed after killing one of her children, she "was not a mad-dog killer. She was very calm. All she said was, 'They will not live like that'.... [S]he decided to kill them and kill herself. That was noble. She was saying, 'I'm a human being. These are my children.'" In using the historical account of Margaret Garner as the beginning point for her story of Sethe—who wants to kill her children to protect them from the system of slavery which dirties, that is, shames, African Americans—Morrison is intent on investigating not only the collective memories of the physical traumas the slaves endured but also the internalized and abiding psychic wounds caused by racial shaming in a white supremacist system of differentiation that imprisons African Americans in what [critic] Robyn Wiegman has aptly described as the "prison-house of epidermal inferiority."

Trauma and Shame Linked

Whereas in *Song of Solomon* Morrison explores the golden legacy of Milkman's racial heritage, which leads back to his slavery roots, in *Beloved*, in contrast, she reveals why the ex-slaves tried to rush away from slavery and the slaves as she describes how the ex-slave Sethe, who lives near Cincinnati in 1873–1874, remains haunted by memories of her slave experiences at the ironically named Kentucky plantation, Sweet Home. In 1855, after the death of her supposedly enlightened and good slave master, Garner, and her mistreatment and humiliation at the hands of Garner's successor, schoolteacher, Sethe makes her difficult flight to freedom only to be tracked down by Schoolteacher one month later, leading to the infanticide and to Sethe's subsequent haunting by the ghost of her dead baby daughter. As Morrison insistently dramatizes the pain and shame endured by Sethe, she depicts the nightmarish world inhabited by victims of trauma, using the device of the ghost to convey the power of trauma to possess and trap its victims. . . .

As Morrison focuses on the physical oppression and also the shame-humiliation suffered by the slaves, she underscores the link between trauma and shame in *Beloved*, showing that, as trauma investigators have concluded, the deliberate and sadistic infliction of injury can induce unbearable and chronic feelings of shame. . . .

White Oppressors to Blame

It is revealing that Morrison herself enacts a rescue-cure of Margaret Garner through her story of Sethe, for as Morrison has admitted, her novelistic "invention" is "much, much happier" than what actually happened to Margaret Garner, who was tried not for the infanticide but for the "*real* crime, which was running away," and who was subsequently returned to slavery. Just as Morrison enacts an authorial rescue of Margaret Garner, so she attempts to work toward a cultural cure in *Beloved* as she examines the painful and secret legacy of slavery and focuses attention on the pernicious effects of internalized racist assumptions about black inferiority on the construction of African-American identities. Continuing the emotional work begun in her earlier novels . . . Morrison explores in *Be-*

loved the painful—and intergenerationally transmitted and in-ternalized—wounds caused by racist oppression, and she works to counteract shame and trauma by establishing an af-fective and cognitive connection with the lost victims of sla-very and by depicting, and in places poetizing, the inner lives of the slaves. Also making a strategic use of a countershaming tactic we have observed Morrison deploy to great effect in her other novels, *Beloved* actively shames the white shamer. There is "no bad luck in the world but white-people," says Baby Suggs, her words exemplary of the way the novel points the finger of blame and shame at the white oppressors who have traumatized and dirtied blacks.

That Sethe kills her infant daughter to prevent her from being defined as racially inferior and animalistic—and thus from being dirtied—underscores the historical shaming of Af-rican slave women that Morrison is intent on exposing in *Beloved.* . . .

Slave Women Were Objects

Affectively and cognitively invested in ripping the veil histori-cally drawn over proceedings too terrible to relate in *Beloved*, Morrison details the oppression of slave women as she tells the story of Sethe, who learns of the shaming power of the white definers: their power to define her as less than human. When the "iron-eyed" and proud Sethe first comes to Sweet Home as a thirteen-year-old, she is left alone by the men, al-lowed to "choose" one of them "in spite of the fact that each one would have beaten the others to mush to have her." "Only my wool shawl kept me from looking like a haint peddling," Sethe remarks, describing the wedding dress she patches to-gether from stolen fabric when she "marries" Halle, Baby Suggs's son. "I wasn't but fourteen years old, so I reckon that's why I was so proud of myself." Yet even as *Beloved* describes Sethe's youthful pride, it also shows that she is implicitly shamed, objectified as the racial and sexual Other—as the animalistic breeder woman. "[M]inus women, fucking cows, dreaming of rape," the Sweet Home men wait for Sethe to select one of them. When Sethe and Halle have sex in the corn-field—Halle wanting "privacy" for Sethe but, instead, getting "public display"—the Sweet Home men, "erect as dogs," watch the corn stalks "dance at noon." To Paul D, the "jump . . . from a calf to a girl wasn't all that mighty," nor was it the "leap Halle believed it would be." Although Sethe has the "amazing luck of six whole years of marriage" to a man who fathers every one of her children, after the death of Garner and the arrival of Schoolteacher, she learns of her value and function as a breeder slave woman, as "property that repro-duced itself without cost."

"It was a book about us but we didn't know that right away," Sethe remarks as she recalls how Schoolteacher asked the Sweet Home slaves questions and then wrote down what they said in his notebook with the ink Sethe mixed for him. Schoolteacher, despite his "pretty manners" and "soft" talking and apparent gentleness, is a cruel racist. A practitioner of the nineteenth-century pseudoscience of race, which included the systematic measurements of facial angles, head shapes, and brain sizes, Schoolteacher is bent, as he makes his "scientific" inquiries, on documenting the racial inferiority of the Sweet Home slaves. At first Sethe is not concerned about Schoolteacher's measuring string. "School-teacher'd wrap that string all over my head, 'cross my nose, around my behind. Number my teeth. I thought he was a fool," she recalls. De-scribing the biosocial investigation of racial difference in the nineteenth century, which was given "political urgency" by the abolitionist movement, Nancy Stepan notes how the "scien-tific" study of race served to "elevate hitherto unconsciously held analogies"—such as the long-standing comparison of blacks to apes—into "self-conscious theory." A theory that codified the shaming of blacks and white contempt for the "lower" races, the study of racial differences functioned to give so-called scientific confirmation of the superiority (pride) of the higher and civilized white race and the inferiority (shame) of the lower and degenerate black race.

Sethe, who initially thinks that Schoolteacher is a fool, is humiliated on discovering the purpose of Schoolteacher's measurements and observations when she overhears him instructing his pupils on how to scientifically describe her as a member of a lower race by listing her human traits on one side of the page and her animal traits on the other. In the essentialist racist discourse of Schoolteacher, Sethe is constructed as animalistic: that is, as fundamentally and biologically different from white people. . . .

Despite her proud demeanor, the "quiet, queenly" Sethe is a woman tormented by humiliated memories not only of how Schoolteacher defined her as animallike but also of how his nephews treated her like an animal. Before Sethe, who is pregnant with Denver, is able to escape from Sweet Home, she has her milk stolen by Schoolteacher's nephews. When Sethe learns from Paul D that her husband, Halle, watched this degrading spectacle and was consequently driven mad by what he had witnessed, her "rebellious" and "greedy" brain takes in this "hateful picture," adding it to her painful memory of this central shame event. "I am full God damn it of two boys with mossy teeth, one sucking on my breast the other holding me down, their book-reading teacher watching and writing it up. . . . Add my husband to it, watching, above me in the loft . . . looking down on what I couldn't look at at all. . . . There is also my husband squatting by the churn smearing the butter as well as its clabber all over his face because the milk they took is on his mind." Objectified as the racial and sexual Other, Sethe is treated like a sexually aggressive wet nurse and mammy when Schoolteacher's nephews sexually assault her in the barn, nursing from her breasts and stealing her milk. She also is treated like an animal, milked as if she were "the cow, no, the goat, back behind the stable because it was too nasty to stay in with the horses." Afterward, she is beaten like an animal by Schoolteacher's nephews for telling Mrs. Garner what has happened to her. Following Schoolteacher's orders, the two boys dig a hole in the ground to protect the developing foetus—which is considered to be the property of the white slave owner—and then they brutally beat Sethe on her back with cowhide. "Felt like I was split in two. . . . Bit a piece of my tongue off when they opened my back. It was hanging by a shred. I didn't mean to. Clamped down on it, it come right off. I thought, Good God, I'm going to eat myself up". . . .

Despite the fact that Sethe is shamed when she is objectified as the sexualized breeder woman and the Jezebel-Mammy, that is, as the sexually aggressive wet nurse, she continues to identify herself primarily as a mother, taking deep pride in her fiercely protective mother love. Indeed, Sethe registers her resistance to the white slave-owner culture through her mothering and her desire to nurse her own children. . . .

At 124 Bluestone Road with Baby Suggs, who was bought out of slavery by her son, Halle, Sethe enjoys twenty-eight days before "the Misery," which is Stamp Paid's term for Sethe's "rough response" to the Fugitive Slave Act of 1850. Sethe has twenty-eight days of happy family and community life, of "having women friends, a mother-in-law, and all her children together; of being part of a neighborhood; of, in fact, having neighbors at all to call her own." When Baby Suggs bathes Sethe's injured body in sections, she attempts to begin the healing of Sethe, who was treated like a fragmented commodity as a slave and dirtied by Schoolteacher. . . .

Dirtied by Whites

Because of community resentment toward the bountiful Baby Suggs, nobody warns Sethe and Baby Suggs of the approach of four white men with the "righteous Look every Negro learned to recognize along with his ma'am's tit," the look that

In this 1937 photograph, British Phrenological Society instructor J.L. Barr demonstrates using a caliper to assess the mental energy in a woman's head. Phrenology, a nineteenth-century pseudoscience based on the belief that a person's character could be revealed by his or her head measurements, resembles the pseudoscience used by Schoolteacher in Morrison's novel Beloved. *© Hulton-Deutsch Collection/Corbis.*

"telegraphed and announced the faggot, the whip, the fist, the lie, long before it went public". . . .

In a maneuver meant to be jarring, *Beloved* locates readers within the shaming perspective of the racist white onlookers—those with the contemptuous "look"—as it provides the first detailed account of the infanticide. . . .

When Sethe commits her act of rough love by slitting the throat of her child with a handsaw, as the circling narrative ultimately discloses, she attempts to protect her children from being dirtied by whites. Her act grows out of her awareness "That anybody white could take your whole self for anything that came to mind. Not just work, kill, or maim you, but dirty you. Dirty you so bad you couldn't like yourself anymore. Dirty you so bad you forgot who you were and couldn't think it up." Sethe wants to protect her children from being victimized by the destructive, dehumanizing forces of slavery and from succumbing to the defining and dirtying power of racist discourse, which constructs white identity as racially and biologically pure and black identity as impure or dirty. "The best thing she was, was her children. Whites might dirty *her* all right, but not her best thing, her beautiful, magical best thing—the part of her that was clean. . . . And no one, nobody on this earth, would list her daughter's characteristics on the animal side of the paper."

Not only is Sethe determined to prevent her children from taking on their prescribed social role as the biologically inferior and racially stigmatized Other, but she also, in attempting to keep her child—the part of her that is clean—from being dirtied, acts to defend against or undo *her own* shame and recover the pride of an idealized self-image. But to Paul D, Sethe, who talks about "safety with a handsaw," does not know "where the world stopped and she began." He tells her that her love is "too thick" and that what she did was "wrong." Insisting that there must have been some other way, he humiliates her in the same way that Schoolteacher did. Revealing his own internalization of Schoolteacher's racist thinking, Paul D compares Sethe to an animal. "You got two feet, Sethe, not four," he tells her, only to later realize how quickly he "had moved from his shame to hers." "Too thick, he said. My love was too thick. What he know about it?" Sethe subsequently says to herself as she justifies her act. "Who in the world is he willing to die for? Would he give his privates to a stranger in return for a carving?" she asks herself, referring to yet another dirtying act she committed: her shameful, Jezebel-like "rutting" with a white stonemason so she could have the word "Beloved" carved on the headstone of her murdered daughter.

Pointing to the narrative's own uncertainties and ambivalences in presenting the infanticide, Sethe's "rough choice" in killing Beloved, a decision that Baby Suggs cannot "approve or condemn," is represented as an act of fierce mother love and resistance to slavery, but also as a brutal act. Sethe tries but is unable to explain to Beloved "what it took to drag the teeth of that saw under the little chin; to feel the baby blood pump like oil in her hands; to hold her face so her head would stay on; to squeeze her so she could absorb, still, the death spasms that shot through that adored body, plump and sweet with life." Repeating a pattern we have observed in other depictions of parental violence in Morrison's novels—such as Cholly's rape of Pecola in *The Bluest Eye* or Eva's murder of Plum in *Sula*—the infanticide mirrors a behavior often found in abusive parents: the mingling of protective with brutal behavior. The infanticide is also explained as an act of revenge against Schoolteacher—as Sethe's determination to "outhurt the hurter," that is, to turn the tables by wounding the wounding Schoolteacher—and as an expression of "rage" that is "prideful, misdirected." Because Sethe's violent act thus reveals her hidden identification with the sadistic white persecutor, Beloved's scarred neck—the mark made by the handsaw Sethe used to slit her daughter's throat—signifies not only the shaming mark or stigma of slavery but also the maternal and intergenerational transmission of black shame and trauma. . . .

The Past Haunts Sethe

Thus Sethe's twenty-eight days of happiness are followed by eighteen years of "disapproval and a solitary life." When Sethe retreats to 124 Bluestone Road after she is released from jail, she defensively withdraws to a walled off and presumably safe place. But the isolated and secretive world she enters affords her little protection against her painful past. That Sethe remains psychically numbed by her slavery past is revealed in the fact that her scarred back, a visible reminder of her persecution as a slave, has no feeling. While Sethe works hard to forget her past, she suffers from rememories, that is spontaneous recurrences of her traumatic and humiliating past. . . .

Caught up in the dialectic of trauma, Sethe lives a constricted, diminished life as she attempts to avoid reminders of and forget the emotional distress of her past and reassert some semblance of control over her inner life. But the past returns to haunt Sethe in the form of the ghost of her dead daughter. . . .

Beloved Is a Complex Figure

Morrison, in describing Beloved's function in the novel, has commented that Beloved, at one and the same time, represents Sethe's resurrected daughter and she also is a survivor from a "true, factual slave ship," who speaks "the language, a traumatized language, of her own experience." That Beloved's traumatized speech—her song—is presented in fragments that readers must carefully reconstruct points to the incipient textual breakdown at this moment of historical recollection and narrative rememory of the collective experience of the Middle Passage. Through the iconic, sensory word-pictures of her monologue, Beloved tells how she and her mother were captured in Africa by white men, "men without skin," and then placed, like human cattle, in a crowded, filthy slave ship where people were forced to crouch in their own excrement and vomit. Locked in traumatic, dissociated memory, the experience remains fixed, frozen in time:

> All of it is now it is always now there will never be a time when I am not crouching and watching others who are crouching too I am always crouching the man on my face is dead. . . . we are all trying to leave our bodies behind the man on my face has done it.

The slave ship was a hellish place of mass suffering and death where the dead remained next to the living for prolonged periods of time, where the men without skin pushed the "hill of dead people" into the sea, and where some captive Africans, like Beloved's mother, who did not like the iron circle around her neck, committed suicide by jumping into the sea. In describing the torments of the slave ships in the traumatized language of Beloved's monologue, the narrative also presents a puzzling, even poetic, text that readers must decode, and thus provides a kind of cognitive-literary shield to protect readers from the abject shame and horror of what is being described. This fragmented narration also enforces reader participation in the careful reconstruction of the trauma- and shame-ridden narrative of the Middle Passage.

Initially, the blissful merging of Sethe and her daughters appears to be healing, a way for Sethe to overcome her traumatic and humiliated rememories. But while Sethe thinks that she can lay down her burdened past and live in peace, she instead becomes involved in a deadly battle for survival. Thus the happy time during which Sethe and her two daughters play together is followed by "furious arguments, the poker slammed up against the wall . . . shouting and crying," which eventually give way to quiet exhaustion as Sethe, Denver, and Beloved become "locked in a love that wore everybody out." . . .

The vicariously shamed and traumatized Denver at first chooses Beloved over Sethe. But over time, as Denver watches Sethe waste away and realizes that her mother might die, she recognizes that she must ask for help from the community. Afraid of the outside world—"Where words could be spoken that would close your ears shut" and where "there were white-people and how could you tell about them?"—a shamefaced and frightened Denver at first walks down the road with lowered head and averted gaze, afraid to look up for fear of encountering white men. Wanting to seek help from someone "who wouldn't shame her on learning that her mother sat around like a rag doll, broke down, finally," Denver eventually finds her way to the home of Lady Jones. That Denver receives assistance from Lady Jones and ultimately from members of the black community, who first provide gifts of food to the starving family and then neighborly support, is suggestive, pointing as it does to the shame-pride script that has governed Sethe's relationship with the community. . . .

Denver as Hope for the Future

In its closing scenes, *Beloved* offers a fictive rescue to its characters and holds out hope for the next generation, embodied in Denver. "I'm proud of her. She turning out fine. Fine," Stamp Paid says of the once shamefaced and traumatized Denver. When Paul D returns to Sethe, who, like Baby Suggs, has retired to her deathbed, he vows to care for her and to bathe her the way Baby Suggs once did in a symbolic attempt to cleanse the dirtied Sethe. Yet even as the narrative acts out a rescue fantasy in this scene, it conveys lingering doubts by having Sethe ask Paul D if he will count her feet, a reference to his insulting remark that she had two feet and not four. The fact that Sethe wonders whether the parts will hold if Paul D washes her in sections also reveals her continuing fear of self-fragmentation. When Paul D tells Sethe that she is her "best thing," her response—"Me? Me?"—at once suggests the potential for healing and yet also leaves open the question of whether Sethe can ever truly recover from her memories and feelings about her traumatic, shame-ridden past. . . .

Intend on memorializing and honoring the lives of the dishonored, disremembered slaves and properly, artistically burying them, Morrison attempts to transform the shame and pain of slavery into artistic pride in *Beloved*. A novel that has achieved a place of honor in the American literary canon, *Beloved* also is a shame- and trauma-saturated work in which Morrison bears witness to the horrors of slavery and rips the veil drawn over proceedings too terrible to relate. Morrison, who gives the literary text as an important site for the production—and potential healing—of African-American culture, speaks the unspeakable in *Beloved* as she dares to penetrate to the dark and disremembered sources of the humiliated and traumatic memories and feelings that continue to haunt the

African-American cultural imagination, like a lingering bad dream, in our race-conscious and race-divided American society.

Morrison Examines the Divisive Impact of Racial Oppression

Babacar M'Baye

Babacar M'Baye is associate professor of African and African American literature and culture at Kent State University in Ohio.

The impact of slavery still reverberates in relations between whites and African Americans, according to M'Baye in the following essay. The concept of racial superiority that was at the heart of slavery continues to create barriers to understanding between the races, asserts M'Baye. In the author's opinion, in Beloved *Toni Morrison exposes the physical and psychological brutality of slavery and racism and celebrates the resilience of African Americans who survived and persevered.*

Set near Cincinnati, Ohio, in 1873, *Beloved* centers on Sethe, a formerly enslaved woman who had escaped from plantation slavery in Kentucky eighteen years earlier. Before her escape, she had sent her three children, two boys and one girl, to 124 Bluestone Road near Cincinnati, Ohio, where Baby Suggs, her free mother-in-law, lived. During her escape—on her way to Ohio—Sethe gave birth to a girl named Denver. Later, the slavemaster tracked her to Bluestone Road. She attempted to kill her children and succeeded in slaying her oldest daughter. She served a jail sentence and returned to 124, where the ghost of her murdered child dwelled for many years. . . .

Babacar M'Baye, *James Baldwin and Toni Morrison: Comparative Critical and Theoretical Essyas*. Basingstoke, Hampshire: Palgrave Macmillan, 2006. Reproduced with permission of Palgrave Macmillan and the author.

Black Women Abused

Beloved examines the psychological and economic effects of slavery on African Americans. In *Beloved*, the effects are visible in the painful memories that Morrison's characters have of slavery. Talking with Beloved and Denver, Sethe tells them about her murdered mother, Nan, who, according to Baby Suggs, lived on a Southern plantation, where the whites raped her and forced her to give up her children. The enslaved black woman who cares for young Sethe explains to her that

> She [Nan] threw them all away but you. The one from the crew she threw away on the island. The others from more whites she also threw away. Without names, she threw them. You she gave the name of the black man. She put her arms around him. The others she did not put her arms around. Never. Never. Telling you. I am telling you, small girl Sethe.

Nan's story is both individual and representative, evidencing repeated instances of her sexual and reproductive exploitation as well as that of enslaved black women in general. . . .

Like Nan, Sethe was a victim of white sexual abuse. Talking to Paul D, who is a long-time friend of Halle, the father of her children, Sethe remembers the day when white men violated her. Sethe describes to Paul D how schoolteacher had sent white men to rape her. Sethe says, "After I left you, those boys came in there and took my milk. That's what they came in there for. Held me down and took it. . . . Schoolteacher made one open up my back, and when it closed it made a tree. It grows there still." The mark of the "tree" on Sethe's back symbolizes the brutal impact of the sexual violence that whites use to dehumanize, depersonalize, and control black people. The whites' selection of Sethe as the object of their sexual violence epitomizes their attempt to subordinate and humiliate not just Sethe, but also the ideals of subversive and resistant blackness and black womanhood that she represents.

After she described the sexual abuse of the whites, Sethe explains to Paul D the impact that such violence might have on Halle. She said,

> They took my milk and he saw it and didn't come down? Sunday came and he didn't. Monday came and no Halle. I thought he was dead, that's why; then I thought they caught him, that's why. Then I thought, No, he's not dead because if he was I'd know of it, and then you come here after all this time and you didn't say he was dead, because you didn't know either.

Sethe did not know that Halle had been forced to watch her being raped, a scene that might have psychologically emasculated him. Paul D tells Sethe: "It broke him, Sethe. . . . You may as well know it all. Last time I saw him he was sitting by the churn. He had butter all over his face." Paul D's confession helps Sethe understand the pain Halle went through before he disappeared. Sethe admits that Halle can never be the same person again after witnessing her abuse: "The milk they took is on his mind." In this sense, she is conscious of the trauma created in the minds of the black men who witnessed the rape of black women. Emasculation is a process in which whites seek to create a false sense of power by humiliating defenseless black men. As Gerda Lerner has shown [in *Black Women in White America: A Documentary History*], whites have historically used abusive methods such as rape in an attempt to maintain a false sense of superiority over black men.

Sethe's attempt to understand Halle's plight suggests her awareness of the connections between the racial oppression of black women and men. As Lerner put it, "Black women have always been more conscious of and more handicapped by race oppression than by sex oppression. They have been subject to all restrictions against Blacks and to those against women. In no area of life have they ever been permitted to attain higher levels of status than white women." Lerner's rationale is corroborated by the discrete social conditions of black and white women in *Beloved*. Neither Sethe nor Baby Suggs have the power of their white mistresses, Mrs. Garner and Mrs. Bodwin, who, in turn, have less power than their husbands do. Yet these white women were shielded from sexual abuse, hard work, and racism.

Additionally, *Beloved* deals with the quandary that African Americans find themselves in when they seek to know which parts of history they should remember. This dilemma is visible when Sethe wants to know and forget about Halle at the same time. Sethe tells herself,

> If he [Halle] was that broken, then, then he is also and certainly dead now. And if Paul D saw him and could not save and comfort him because the iron bit was in his mouth, then there is still more that Paul D could tell me and my brain would go right ahead and take it and never say, No thank you. I don't want to know or have to remember that.

Yet the narrator tells us that "her brain was not interested in the future. Loaded with the past and hungry for more, it left her no room to imagine, let alone plan for, the next day." Sethe's double consciousness reveals the difficulty of selecting which parts of the past to remember when history is fragmented into discrete pieces. . . .

Whites Made Freedom Elusive

In *Beloved*, the theorizing of whiteness is apparent when Baby Suggs condemns whites for perpetuating injustices on blacks. Baby Suggs tells Sethe: "Those white things have taken all I had or dreamed . . . and broke my heartstrings too. There is no bad luck in the world but whitefolks." Baby Suggs is saddened by her memories of her children who were taken away from her during slavery.

> Thwarted yet wondering, she chopped away with the hoe. What could it be? This dark and coming thing. What was left to hurt her now? News of Halle's death? No. She had

been prepared for that better than she had for his life. The last of her children, whom she barely glanced at when he was born because it wasn't worth the trouble to try to learn features you would never see change into adulthood anyway.

Baby Suggs's views on whiteness are also evident in her recollection of the experiences she and her son Halle had in Sweet Home. Baby Suggs served at Sweet Home for ten years as both a cook and a fieldworker until Halle bought her freedom by hiring out years of his Sundays. Mr. Garner, the owner of Sweet Home, made arrangements with Mr. and Mrs. Bodwin, two humanitarian abolitionists who offered to give Baby Suggs a home in exchange for menial work: "Baby Suggs agreed to the situation, sorry to see the money go but excited about a house with steps—never mind she couldn't climb them. Mr. Garner told the Bodwins that she was a right fine cook as well as a fine cobbler and showed his belly and the sample on his feet. Everybody laughed." Baby Suggs then believed that the slaves of the Garners would soon be free. Her expectation was marred when, after the death of Mr. Garner, his brother-in-law—whom Sethe and the others nicknamed "schoolteacher"—imposed tough laws at Sweet Home. Morrison writes,

> Voices remind schoolteacher about the spoiling these particular slaves have had at Garner's hands. There's laws against what he done: letting niggers hire out their own time to buy themselves. He even let em have guns! And you think he mated them niggers to get him some more? Hell no! He planned for them to marry! If that don't beat it all! Schoolteacher sighs, and says doesn't he know it? He had come to put the place aright.

Halle had also made arrangements to purchase his own freedom for $123.70, the equivalent of one year of debt work, but schoolteacher put a stop to the practice of hiring out time. Halle tells Sethe, "Schoolteacher in there told me to quit it. Said the reason for doing it don't hold. I should do the extra but here at Sweet Home.... The question now is, Who's going buy you [Sethe] out? Or me? Or her [Beloved]?". Schoolteacher's fear of black freedom led him to become racist, paranoid, and violent toward blacks. Accusing a slave called Sixo of stealing, "Schoolteacher beat him anyway to show him that definitions belonged to the definers—not the defined." These incidents show that the white promise of freedom was unreal, and that the limited freedom of blacks was not given; it was paid for.

The illusive nature of the white promise of freedom is also noticeable in a dialogue in which Sethe and Baby Suggs express their differing views about whites. In this exchange of ideas, Baby Suggs develops a premise that counters each of the hypotheses that Sethe makes about whites. The dialogue reads as follows:

"They got me out of jail," Sethe once told Baby Suggs.

"They also put you in it," she answered.

"They drove you 'cross the river."

"On my son's back."

"They gave you this house."

"Nobody *gave* me nothing."

"I got a job from them."

"He got a cook from them, girl."

"Oh, some of them do right by us."

"And every time it's a surprise, ain't it?"

"You didn't used to talk this way."

"Don't box with me. There's more of us drowned than there is all of them ever lived from the start of time."

This passage shows the discrepancies between Sethe's and Baby Suggs's opinions about freedom and white people. Unlike Sethe, Baby Suggs perceives freedom as a result of black struggles rather than of white benevolence. Unlike Sethe, who distinguishes between good and bad white people, Baby Suggs sees no variation among whites. Furthermore, unlike Sethe, who expresses gratitude to the white people who helped her get out of jail, Baby Suggs conveys no appreciation for any white person. Baby Suggs's opinions about whites diverge from those of Sethe mainly because Baby Suggs believes that the limited freedom she has was wrested from whites; it was not handed down to her. Being more mature and experienced than Sethe, Baby Suggs is able to see white people as part of a collective system of oppression from which freedom is to be taken, not granted. . . .

Debunking White Supremacy

Finally, *Beloved* is a critique of the white American ideology of racial supremacy. This critique is visible when schoolteacher develops racist attitudes toward blacks. Expressing the scientific racism that was popular in the second half of the nineteenth century, schoolteacher views black people as members of an inferior race who need to be saved from barbarity through exposure to white civilization. When he sees that Sethe has tried to kill her children, he thinks to himself, "All testimony to the results of a little so-called freedom imposed on people who needed every care and guidance in the world to keep them from the cannibal life they preferred." In order to understand schoolteacher's racism, one must analyze the theory that Stamp Paid, the black man who helped Sethe escape to Ohio, develops about the white imagination of blackness. Stamp Paid's theory is as follows:

> Whitepeople believed that whatever the manners, under every dark skin was a jungle. Swift unnavigable waters, swinging screaming baboons, sleeping snakes, red gums ready for

their sweet white blood. In a way, he thought, they were right. The more colored people spent their strength trying to convince them how gentle they were, how clever and loving, how human, the more they used themselves up to persuade whites of something Negroes believed could not be questioned, the deeper and more tangled the jungle grew inside. But it wasn't the jungle blacks brought with them to this place from the other (livable) place. It was the jungle whitefolks planted in them. And it grew. It spread. In, through and after life, it spread, until it invaded the whites who had made it. Touched them every one. Changed and altered them. Made them bloody, silly, worse than even they wanted to be, so scared were they of the jungle they had made. The screaming baboon lived under their own white skin; the red gums were their own. . . .

Morrison depicts the theorizing of whiteness in American culture as a delusion. In *Playing in the Dark*, she writes: "Because they appear almost always in conjunction with representations of black or Africanist people who are dead, impotent, or under control, these images of blinding whiteness seem to function as both antidote for and meditation on the shadow that is companion to this whiteness—a dark and abiding presence that moves the hearts and texts of American literature with fear and longing." . . . This American Africanist construct is what *Beloved* . . . dismantled by exposing the scars of slavery and racism on the American psyche.

Slavery Damaged the Mother-Child Relationship

Wilfred D. Samuels and Clenora Hudson-Weems

Wilfred D. Samuels is associate professor of English and ethnic studies at the University of Utah. Clenora Hudson-Weems is a professor of English at the University of Missouri–Columbia.

Beloved *differs from traditional slave narratives in that it addresses topics considered too unspeakable to be retold, assert Samuels and Hudson-Weems in the following essay. In particular, in* Beloved *Toni Morrison explores the reality of what it was like to be a female slave, as most slave narratives were told from a masculine perspective, the authors point out. According to Samuels and Hudson-Weems, under slavery black women had no right to their children, who were the property of the slave owners. This often resulted in children and their mothers being separated, with devastating psychological consequences, they argue.*

Six years in the making, *Beloved* artistically dramatizes a haunting amalgam of the past and present experiences of an escaped female slave, Sethe, tracing the heroine's quest for meaning and wholeness in slavery and in freedom. Ever present as a reminder of the past is Beloved, the ghost spirit of Sethe's slave child, whom Sethe killed by slashing her throat with a handsaw in what she considered a mercy killing. After haunting her mother's home at 124 Bluestone Road for more than eighteen years, the ghost becomes flesh and, in the guise of a twenty-year-old woman-child (the same age Beloved would have been had she lived), walks into Sethe's house, where she becomes the manifestation of her mother's conscience.

Wilfred D. Samuels and Clenora Hudson-Weems, *Toni Morrison*. Belmont, CA: Twayne Publishers, 1990. Reproduced by permission of Gale, a part of Cengage Learning.

In committing her brutal act, Sethe believed she was sparing the child from the "unspeakable" fate to which most female slaves were heiresses, a deplorable fate breeding abundant tragic consequences. Morrison's characters are well aware of the vulnerable position in which the black slave woman has been placed: "That anybody white could take your whole self for anything that came to mind. Not just work, kill or maim you. Dirty you so bad you couldn't like yourself anymore."

The Source of the Story

Set in the nineteenth century, primarily in the gruesome pre– and post–Civil War era, *Beloved* is developed through a series of flashbacks. The recollections are triggered when Paul D, a fellow slave from the Sweet Home Plantation, walks back into Sethe's life. But they are also mandated by Sethe's "rememory," a memory "loaded with the past." In spite of her effort to beat back the past, she is unable to transcend it: "Some things you forget. Other things you never do." . . .

Beloved is an historical novel, framed in purpose, thematics, and structure after the African-American slave narrative. Like the paradigmatic *The Narrative of Frederick Douglass, An American Slave* (1847) and *Incidents in the Life of a Slave Girl* (1861), this novel offers the personal accounts of "black slaves and ex-slaves of their experiences in slavery and of their efforts to obtain freedom [as described by Frances Smith Foster in *Witnessing Slavery: The Development of Antebellum Slave Narratives*]." Although *Beloved* is specifically Sethe's story, it is also the story of all the slaves of the Sweet Home Plantation of Kentucky: Baby Suggs, Paul D Garner, Paul F Garner, Paul A Garner, Halle Suggs, and Sixo. Thus, it is also, like the major works of the slave narrative genre, the composite story of all slaves and their quest for freedom through flight.

Unlike other significant texts that belong to this unique American genre, *Beloved* requires no call for the abolition of slavery. This is because Sethe's story is narrated to a twentieth-century audience. Nevertheless, in the tradition of this art form *Beloved* successfully chronicles incidents in the exslave's mind, providing the reader with insights not only into Sethe's thoughts and actions but also into the structure and workings of the plantocracy that denied her basic human and political rights. Thus, as is true of the more traditional slave narrative, *Beloved* records the cruelty, violence, and degradation—whether the physical floggings or the psychological fragmentation of the black family—that often victimized slaves, irrespective of age or gender. . . .

The Motives for the Telling

What concerns Morrison in *Beloved*, however, is not what history has recorded in the slave narratives but what it has omitted. Foster offers insight into the significant dilemma of the slave narrator who, in the effort to harness support for the abolition of slavery, did not wish to offend the audience. This made compromises necessary. According to Foster, "The nature of these compromises determined the form and content of the narratives." Fundamentally, she continues, "the narrator's fidelity to the reality of the American slave experience was at the risk of offending many Americans who, regardless of their humanitarian beliefs, were, after all, members of the society being criticized. Moreover, the narratives ran the risk of alienating segments of people because the accounts of slavery presented an unsavory view of the South in particular and the United States in general." The caution practiced by the slave narrator was inevitable.

Morrison's awareness of this tempered voice resonates in her conviction that "whatever the level or eloquence or the form [of the slave narrative], popular taste discouraged the writers from dwelling too long or too carefully on the more sordid details of their experience." But, she argued, by "taking refuge in the literary convention of the day," the slave narrator would often "pull the narrative up short."

As Morrison would have Sethe reveal, however, there was another reason behind the careful selection of the events that they would record and the "careful rendering of those that they chose to describe": "every mention of [the] past life hurt. Everything in it was painful or lost." Consequently, Sethe and "Baby Suggs had agreed without saying so that [the past] was unspeakable." Although she would often provide Denver, who yearned for a knowledge of her mother's past, with some information, "Sethe gave short replies or rambling incomplete reveries."

For Morrison the cost of this blocking was exorbitant in the long run. Thus, like the slave narrator who called for the abolition of slavery, Morrison's purpose in *Beloved* is corrective. Through her narrator she aims to expose the wrong and rectify the full story. Conceding that "somebody forgot to tell somebody something," Morrison states, "My job becomes how to rip that veil" behind which the slave narrator was forced to hide. But this resolution necessarily requires that she "depend upon the recollection of others," that she draw upon the "memories within."

For Morrison this is the significant act of "rememory": "a journey to a site to see what remains have been left behind and to reconstruct the world that these remains imply." Ultimately, then, she seeks in *Beloved* to find and expose a truth about "the interior life of people who didn't write it (which doesn't mean that they didn't have it)"; to "fill in the blanks that the slave narrative left"; to "part the veil that was frequently drawn"; and to "implement the stories that [she had] heard."

What Morrison also unearths at the excavation site is the silenced voice of the black slave woman, for more often than not her story had been told by the black male narrator whose focus was primarily upon his own journey to wholeness. Although the women who appear are not mere fixtures, for through them the horrors of slavery are unravelled, what is generally told is his/tory rather than her/story; her dimmed voice left her to live a life of quiet desperation. . . .

A Search for Wholeness

Morrison's *Beloved* . . . provides the avenue for a resurrected female slave narrator's voice. And it is not only Sethe who speaks: it is her mother; Patsy, "the Thirty-mile Woman"; and Sethe's two girl-women, Denver and Beloved. Above all, one hears the haunting voice of Baby Suggs, whose broken hip is the physical legacy of sixty years of bondage and whose final escape into colors is the only peace she had known in slavery or in freedom. Barbara Christian correctly notes [in "From the Inside Out"] that "Afro-American women writers rewrite the established history by embodying their ancestors' memory in fiction, and as well respond to previous Afro-American women's literature. Contemporary Afro-American women's work then is intertextual as well as reiteration of the restriction based on class, race, gender, imposed on their forebears."

It is within the realm of the black women novelists' effort to literally reclaim their history by writing, to borrow from Christian, "from the inside out," that Morrison's treatment of Sethe's quest for wholeness must be first understood. Paradoxically, Sethe initially appears to be without a sense of liminality [being on the threshold of passing from one state to another]. This is due primarily to the untraditional behavior of the Garners, who "ran a special kind of slavery" on their Sweet Home Plantation, where there were no "men-bred slaves." Mrs. Garner, who "hummed when she worked," and Mr. Garner, who "acted like the world was a toy he was supposed to have fun with," treated their slaves "like paid labor, listening to what they said, teaching what they wanted known." The Sweet Home men, we are told, are "Men every one."

But Sethe's inability to recall much of her life before age thirteen, the point at which she came to Sweet Home to replace the recently freed Baby Suggs, suggests that her lack of liminality is counterfeit; it is due in part to her successful act of "disremembering," of consciously obliterating her painful past. Most painful had been the denial and then severance of any semblance of a meaningful relationship with her mother, who had been branded and later hanged because of her daily resistance to slavery. . . .

With the death of Mr. Garner and the coming of his brother, schoolteacher, and his nephews, however, Sethe becomes aware of her own liminality as she is made to realize that Sweet Home is "a wonderful lie." . . .

Sethe's liminality is intensified with her growing awareness or her personal status as chattel. It begins when she accidentally overhears a discussion between schoolteacher and his nephews in which he denigrates her humanity by telling his nephews to "put her [Sethe's] human characteristics on the left; her animal ones on the right." . . .

Amidst the deterioration of black life on Sweet Home, Sethe succeeds in getting her children on board the northbound caravan. Before she can join them, however, she becomes the sport of schoolteacher's assistants, who violate Sethe by stealing the milk she bears because of her pregnancy with her fourth child. She is brutally beaten for reporting this heinous crime to Mrs. Garner. Pregnant, barefoot, and mutilated, Sethe escapes to Ohio, to her mother-in-law, Baby Suggs, and her children, including her "crawling—already?" baby girl, Beloved. Although Sethe does not arrive in Cincinnati with Halle, she arrives with Denver, her fourth child, who was born en route.

In her narrative of Sethe's liminality and flight to freedom, Morrison returns to the site of Sethe's rememory to excavate its hidden treasures, painful though they may be. Successfully ripping the veil to reach the level that was "loaded with the past," Morrison finds among the ruins of the slave experience the often forgotten instrumental roles and places slave women played and occupied. Significantly, her find includes the seminal role they played, for example, in the historical caravan to freedom, the underground railroad. By having a woman conductor convey Sethe's three children north to freedom, Morrison reestablishes the role of women in this historically significant avenue of escape. . . .

Sethe Is a Mother Figure

Married by age fourteen, Sethe was pregnant with her fourth child by age nineteen. Although Sweet Home's Garner prided himself on the fact that his male slaves were men, and not "men-bred slaves," Mrs. Garner betrayed the owners' hidden agenda, revealing that the most important purpose of the slave woman was childbearing. When Sethe informs Mrs. Garner that she plans to marry Halle, Mrs. Garner asks, "Are you already expecting?" When Sethe responds in the negative, Mrs. Garner informs her, "Well, you will be. You know that, don't you?" Sethe had in fact been brought to Sweet Home to serve as much as a sexual mate to any one of the Sweet Home men of her choosing as she had been brought to replace Baby Suggs, who was now too old to either work in the field or reproduce.

That schoolteacher values Sethe for her childbearing capabilities, and thus for the capital she represents, is indicated both by his decision to capture her and return her to slavery and by the punishment that he meted out to his nephew, whom he blames for overheating his prized woman slave, leading her to escape. "Schoolteacher had chastised that nephew, telling him to think—just think—what would his own horse do if you beat it beyond the point of education. Or Chipper, or Samson. Suppose you beat the hounds past that point thataway." Sethe comes to realize that it was her apparent value as "property that reproduced itself without cost" that had allowed her to enjoy the benefit of a pastoral life on Sweet Home.

If the most important factor impairing the mobility of fugitive slave women was their concern with the welfare of their children, as Deborah White suggests [in *Ar'n't I a Woman? Female Slaves in the Plantation South*], then the reverse is equally significant in their decision to flee: They did so to ensure their children's welfare. This is the impetus for Sethe. Separated for the first time from her children, especially her infant "crawling already? girl," Beloved, Sethe, who according to Paul D was driven by a love that was "too thick," struggles to reach Cincinnati at any cost. . . .

With Sethe and Beloved, however, Morrison probes deeper into the psychological network and nature of nursing and the mother-infant bond—the social and emotional relationship between mother and infant—that is its inevitable outcome. Morrison suggests that such a bond is fundamental to the psychological development of both mother and child. Exploring this relationship within the context of a particular historical period and social arrangement—slavery—she addresses yet another of her finds at the excavation site of Sethe's memory: the psychological damage of slavery to the mother-child relationship.

Morrison's examination heightens the intensity of the damage done to this almost instinctive relationship because both children, Denver and Beloved, unlike Milkman and Son, are in their infancy, and they are girls; the mother/daughter relationship is of paramount importance to the socialization process. To compound it, Sethe, the mother figure, is a mere girl herself. Unlike Ruth or Therese, Sethe is a woman-child of nineteen. Having herself been robbed of this crucial bond with her own mother, Sethe is intimately familiar with the psychological devastation her baby girls would be subjected to without her milk. . . .

In treating the theme of the great mother, as nurturant and nursing figure, whose primary responsibility is that of caring for her children, Morrison returns to the concomitant image of the archetypal "terrible mother" as well; for Sethe, like Eva who murders Plum [in Morrison's book *Sula*], is a mother who kills her child in order to save its life, or give it new life. Sethe's original intention was to kill all four of her children, not just one. Upon seeing the slave catchers and schoolteacher's hat, Sethe automatically knew that returning to slavery was not an alternative: Her children, now free, would not become slaves again. "I couldn't let all that [the brief freedom they had known] go back, and I couldn't let her [Beloved] nor any of 'em live under schoolteacher." Death, she was convinced, would provide a life that was better than anything she had known or experienced at Sweet Home. . . .

We must not ignore that Sethe sees her children as her property; each one is a "life she had made"; each had "all the parts of her." Thus perceived, Sethe's actions become more complex. Indeed, she allows us to frame the larger question here that Morrison seems to have ignored in *Sula:* Does a mother have the right to take the life of her child? The answer is not cut-and-dried in *Beloved,* especially since Morrison includes the powerful suggestion, through Sethe's mother's experience, that the slave child who was born was in fact wanted by its mother. This, one may argue, leads to the even more powerful conclusion that "most children born . . . are born as the realization of the instinctual wishes of their mother."

To be sure, we find in Sethe's behavior yet another example of the slave's resistance to slavery; for though the North American annals of slavery record, relatively speaking, offer few collective and even revolutionary acts of resistance, more were, as Deborah White points out, "generally individualistic, and aimed at maintaining what the slave master and overseer had in the course of their relationships, perceived as acceptable level of work, shelter, force, punishment, and free time . . . the best most could hope for was survival with a modicum of dignity." . . .

Given the primacy of childbearing to the perpetuation of slavery, however, the bondswoman had, through her reproductive capacity, yet another avenue of resistance; and as records of feigned illness, deliberate and nondeliberate miscarriage, and self-imposed sterility indicate, they found and took advantage of these avenues of resistance. Although infanticide represented, according to White, an "atypical behavior on the part of the slave mothers," it was nevertheless an avenue that was available and used by some. . . .

For Sethe, the dilemma is embodied in the very question of motherhood, which requires not only that one be "good enough, alert enough, strong enough" but also that one "stay alive just that much longer." Unless a mother remained carefree, she concluded, "mother love was a killer." The complexity of Sethe's rich, ironic statement should not be overlooked. For her, motherlove is, literally and figuratively speaking, a "killer." Her dilemma emerges essentially from the diametrically opposing views of relationship that the system of slavery demanded and fostered, one grounded in separation of families, and one—sacred to Sethe—grounded in a sense of correctness. Concerned only with its own perpetuation, slavery stood in contradiction to Sethe's ideal of care. She confesses, "I wouldn't draw breath without my children"; and she asks, "nobody's ma'am could run off and leave her daughter, would she?" Clearly, Sethe defines and perceives herself firmly in terms of a world of care and protection for her children. . . .

Economic Slavery the Real Evil

Morrison never ceases to hold before us the environment that created Sethe: economic slavery. It alone remains the source, the context, of her madness—the impetus for her irrational behavior. Interestingly enough, it is Paul D who is able to understand and verbalize Sethe's dilemma. He concludes, "for a used-to-be-slave woman to love anything that much was dangerous, especially if it was her children she had settled on to love." Here Paul D points to the tension created by the system of slavery and the maternal instinct of the slave woman. Slavery claimed ownership of all of its property, irrespective of age and gender, including the siblings of its female slaves. Simultaneously, the slave mother instinctively sought to hold on to her progeny.

Social Issues in Literature

CHAPTER 3

Contemporary Perspectives on Slavery

Slavery Remains a Significant Global Problem

E. Benjamin Skinner, as told to Terrence McNally

E. Benjamin Skinner is a journalist and author of A Crime So Monstrous: Face-to-Face with Modern-Day Slavery. *A journalist and radio host, Terrence McNally writes, consults, and gives speeches on issues of social responsibility and sustainable development.*

There are 27 million people in slavery today—more than at any other time in history, Skinner reports in the following article. Today's slaves are cheap and disposable compared with US slaves prior to the Civil War, Skinner contends. In the nineteenth century, a healthy male slave would cost the equivalent today of forty thousand dollars. In contrast, slaves today can be bought for as little as fifty dollars, he reveals.

The world suffers global recession, enormous inequity, hunger, deforestation, pollution, climate change, nuclear weapons, terrorism, etc. To those who say we're not really making progress, many might point to the fact that at least we've eliminated slavery.

But sadly that is not the truth.

Millions Are in Slavery Today

One hundred forty-three years after passage of the 13th Amendment to the U.S. Constitution and 60 years after Article 4 of the U.N.'s Universal Declaration of Human Rights banned slavery and the slave trade worldwide, there are more slaves than at any time in human history—27 million.

E. Benjamin Skinner interviewed by Terrence McNally, "There Are More Slaves Today than at Any Time in Human History," *Alternet*, 2009. Alternet.org. Reproduced by permission.

Today's slavery focuses on big profits and cheap lives. It is not about owning people like before, but about using them as completely disposable tools for making money.

During the four years that Benjamin Skinner researched modern-day slavery, he posed as a buyer at illegal brothels on several continents, interviewed convicted human traffickers in a Romanian prison and endured [infection with the parasite] giardia, malaria, dengue [fever] and a bad motorcycle accident.

But Skinner is most haunted by his experience in a brothel in Bucharest, Romania, where he was offered a young woman with Down syndrome in exchange for a used car. . . .

Terrence McNally: What first got you interested in slavery?

Benjamin Skinner: The fuel began before I was born. The abolitionism in my blood began at least as early as the 18th century, when my Quaker ancestors stood on soapboxes in Connecticut and railed against slavery. I had other relatives that weren't Quaker, but had the same beliefs. My great-great-great-grandfather fought with the Connecticut artillery, believing that slavery was an abomination that could only be overturned through bloodshed.

Yet today, after the deaths of 360,000 Union soldiers, after over a dozen conventions and 300 international treaties, there are more slaves than at any point in human history.

Is that raw numbers or as a percentage of the population?

I want to be very clear what I mean when I say the word slavery. If you look it up in Webster's dictionary, the first definition is "drudgery or toil." It's become a metaphor for undue hardship, because we assume that once you legally abolish something, it no longer exists. But as a matter of reality for up to 27 million people in the world, slaves are those forced to work, held through fraud, under threat of violence, for no pay beyond subsistence. It's a very spare definition.

Whose definition is that?

Kevin Bales's. [His *Disposable People: New Slavery in the Global Economy* was nominated for the 1999 Pulitzer Prize, and he is the president of Free the Slaves] I'm glad you asked because he's not given enough credit. He originally came up with the number 27 million, and it's subsequently been buttressed by international labor organization studies. Governments will acknowledge estimates of some 12.3 million slaves in the world, but NGOs [nongovernmental organizations] in those same countries say the numbers are more than twice as high.

Kevin did a lot of the academic work that underpinned my work. I wanted to go out and get beyond the numbers, to show what one person's slavery meant. In the process of doing that, I met hundreds of slaves and survivors.

Disposable People

As an investigative reporter rather than an academic, you take us where the trades are made, the suffering takes place and the survivors eke out their existences.

In an underground brothel in Bucharest, I was offered a young woman with the visible effect of Down syndrome. One of her arms was covered in slashes, where I can only assume she was trying to escape daily rape the only way she knew how. That young woman was offered to me in trade for a used car.

This was a Romanian used car?

Yes, and I knew that I could get that car for about 1,500 euros. While that may sound like a very low price for human life, consider that five hours from where I live in New York—a three-hour flight down to Port au Prince, Haiti, and an hour from the airport—I was able to negotiate for a 10-year-old girl for cleaning and cooking, permanent possession and sexual favors. What do you think the asking price was?

I don't know . . . $7,500?

They asked for $100, and I talked them down to $50. Now to put that in context: Going back to the time when my abolitionist ancestors were on their soapbox, in 1850, you could buy a healthy grown male for the equivalent of about $40,000.

When I first read such big numbers, I was shocked.

This is not to diminish the horrors that those workers would face, nor to diminish their dehumanization one bit. It was an abomination then as it is today. But in the mid-19th century, masters viewed their slaves as an investment.

But here's the thing: When a slave costs $50 on the street in broad daylight in Port au Prince—by the way, this was in a decent neighborhood, everybody knew where these men were and what they did—such people are, to go back to Kevin's term, eminently disposable in the eyes of their masters.

If my reading is correct, the biggest concentrations of the slave trade are in Southeast Asia and portions of Latin America?

If you were to plot slaves on the map, you'd stick the biggest number of pins in India, followed by Pakistan, Nepal, Bhutan. There are arguably more slaves In India than the rest of the world combined.

And yet, if you look at international efforts or American pressure, India is largely let off the hook because Indian federal officials claim, "We have no slaves. These are just poor people. And these exploitive labor practices,"—if you're lucky enough to get that term out of them—"are a byproduct of poverty."

Let me be clear, the end of slavery cannot wait for the end of poverty. Slavery in India is primarily generational debt bondage, people whose grandparents took a debt.

To go back to the definition: Forced to work against their will with no escape.

Held through fraud under threat of violence for no pay beyond subsistence. These are people that cannot walk away.

I stumbled upon a fellow in a quarry in Northern India who'd been enslaved his entire life. He had assumed that slavery at birth. His grandfather had taken a debt of 62 cents, and three generations and three slave masters later, the principal had not been paid off one bit. The family was illiterate and innumerate. This fellow, who I call Gonoo—he asked me to protect his identity—was still forced to work, held through fraud under threat of violence for no pay beyond subsistence.

Since he was a child, he and his family and his children, along with the rest of the enslaved villagers, took huge rocks out of the earth. They pummeled those rocks into gravel for the subgrade of India's infrastructure, which is the gleaming pride of the Indian elites.

They further pulverized that gravel into silica sand for glass. There's only one way that you turn a profit off hand-made sand, and that's through slavery.

Another method you describe: Someone shows up in a poverty-stricken village saying they need workers for the mines hundreds of miles away.

It's a massive problem in the north of Brazil. What's tricky about this, in many cases these workers want to work. But they don't want to be forced to work under threat of violence, beaten regularly, having the women in their lives raped as a means of humiliating them, and then not being paid anything.

They are transported to the mines, and when they arrive, they have a debt for that transportation, which is greater than anything they will ever be able to repay.

And if they try to leave, there are men with guns. That's slavery. In the Western Hemisphere, child slavery, as we spoke of before, is most rampant in Haiti. According to UNICEF [the United Nations Children's Fund], there are 300,000 child slaves in Haiti.

Does that mean in Haiti or originating in Haiti?

That means within Haitian borders.

So with all the poverty in Haiti, there are still people who can afford 300,000 slaves?

Well if they're paying $50 ...

I went back last summer with Dan Harris of ABC *Nightline*. He was pretty incredulous of my claim. In fact, it ended up taking him 10 hours from ABC's offices in Manhattan, but by the end of those 10 hours, he'd negotiated with not one, but three traffickers who'd offered him three separate girls.

As he put it, the remarkable thing is not that you can get a child for $50, but that you can get a child for free. When you go up into these villages, you see such desperation on the parts of the parents.

I want to make clear, I never paid for human life; I never would pay for human life. I talked to too many individuals who run trafficking shelters and help slaves become survivors. They implored me, "Do not pay for human life. You will be giving rise to a trade in human misery, and as a journalist, you'll be projecting to the world that this is the way that you own the problem." If you were to buy all 300,000 child slaves in Haiti, next year, you'd have 600,000.

Buying Slaves Their Freedom

If you were to buy the 300,000 slaves in Haiti in one fell swoop, you would be telling traders, "Hey, business is good," and so they'd grab more slaves.

You're talking about introducing hard currency into a transaction that in many cases hasn't involved hard currency in the past. You're massively incentivizing a trade in human lives.

These are those who practice what they call redemptions, buying slaves their freedom. Who's doing it, and what's your analysis of it?

On the basis of three months spent in southern and northern Sudan, two months in southern Sudan in particular.... There was one particular evangelical group based in Switzer-

This February 2011 photograph portrays Pakistani debt-bonded laborers breathing thick dust as they make bricks, struggling to repay the kiln owner for an advance (peshgi) they were forced to take. An estimated 1.8 million Pakistani brick makers are trapped in this peshgi system, often for generations. © Michael Coyne/Corbis.

land, organized and run by an American who raised cash around the States. They'd go to a Sunday School or a second-grade class in Colorado, talk about slavery, and say, "Bring us your lunch money. If you can get us $50, we will buy a slave's freedom."

It was a very effective sales pitch. They managed to raise over $3 million dollars by my calculations over the course of the 1990s.

In theory, they were giving money to "retrievers" who would go into northern Sudan, and through whatever means necessary, secure the slaves' freedom and bring them back down into the south.

In the context of the Sudanese civil war, slavery is used as a weapon of war by the north. Northern militias raid southern villages, and in many cases, kill the men and take the women and children as slaves and as a weapon of genocide. That much is not questioned. There is no question that these slave raids were going on.

I found that redemption on the ground was enormously problematic. There was scant oversight. They were literally giving duffel bags full of cash to factions within the rebels that were at that point resisting an ongoing peace process.

What they risked doing, whether through recklessness or through intent, was to become essentially angels of destruction at a time when a negotiated peace was just beginning to take hold. Thankfully, at this point they've scaled back the redemptions.

So they were collecting money in the States to free slaves, and then funding a rebel movement in a war, and . . .

Potentially prolonging the war.

Thankfully, in the end, the death of rebel leader John Gurang meant that a different faction came to be more powerful. From my perspective, however, what was going on there was largely fraudulent.

I went back and asked the rebel officials, "What do you do with this money?" and they said, "We use it for the benefit of the people." Which begs the question, "But I thought this was being used to buy back slaves. I don't get it."

And they said, "Well you know, there's clothes, uniforms . . ." They didn't actually say arms, but they said all sorts of things that they needed hard currency for, and this was their way of getting the cash.

I don't blame the rebels. If I were in a similar situation, I'd probably do the same thing. The most important point is this: By the merest estimates there are still some 12,000 slaves held in brutal bondage in the north of Sudan, and the government has not arrested or prosecuted one slave raider, one slave trader, one slave master. And as long as that continues to be the situation, the government of Sudan is in gross violation of international law.

All Slavery Is Wrong

How does the distinction between sexual slavery and other sorts of labor show up, and how does it matter?

When we're defining slavery, fundamentally at its core it's the same in each and every circumstance. We're talking about people forced to work, held through fraud, under threat of violence, for no pay beyond subsistence. If we're talking about forced commercial sexual slavery, forced prostitution, there's an added element of humiliation or shame, because we're talking about rape.

In many parts of the world and in many traditional societies, if a woman is raped it's her fault. If a woman is liberated and tries to go back to the village she comes from, she will never again lead a normal life.

I think it's safe to say even in the United States, which we assume is a much more welcoming, tolerant society, women who've been in prostitution, regardless if it's forced or not, have a difficult time leading a normal life afterward.

There is a school of thought that sexual slavery is somehow worse than other forms of slavery. I actually don't buy that. I think that all slavery is monstrous, and no one slave's emancipation should wait for that of another. At the same time, if some people are moved to fight sexual slavery and sexual trafficking at the exclusion of other forms of slavery, God bless them, as long as they're fighting slavery at the end of the day.

Briefly, what is the situation in America?

On average, in the past half-hour, one more person will have been trafficked to the United States into slavery. About 14,000–17,000 are trafficked into the U.S. each year and forced to work within U.S. borders under threat of violence for no pay beyond subsistence.

US Companies Are Complicit in Modern-Day Slavery

Sarah C. Pierce

Sarah C. Pierce was a student writer for the Journal of Gender, Race and Justice *when she wrote this piece.*

Although the Trafficking Victims Protection Act makes it illegal to engage in human trafficking in the United States, in reality few individuals and even fewer corporations are prosecuted for violations or complicity in violations, Pierce contends in the following essay. Corporations that engage in human trafficking typically use subcontractors to avoid prosecution, Pierce asserts. Congress should change the law to make corporations legally responsible for labor all the way down their supply chains, she argues.

Moises and Maria Rodriguez lived in Hudson, Colorado with their son, Javier Rodriguez, nearby. Together, the family operated a successful business: Moises was well known in northern Colorado as a "contractor" who could supply crews for farm work, Maria managed the books, and Javier supervised workers at the labor camp. One of Moises' customers was Grant Family Farms, one of Colorado's best-known organic farms. The seemingly thriving family business, however, covered an elaborate scheme in which migrants were smuggled to the camp, imposed with a debt for their transportation, and forced to endure an "uninhabitable" living situation and constant fear of deportation. Agents with U.S. Immigration and Customs Enforcement discovered the camp in October 2004. The family pled guilty to harboring and smuggling mi-

Sarah C. Pierce, "Turning a Blind Eye: U.S. Corporate Involvement in Modern-Day Slavery," *Journal of Gender, Race & Justice*, vol. 14, September 2011. Reproduced by permission.

grant workers in May 2006. That same year, the victims filed a private federal lawsuit against both the Rodriguez family and Grant Family Farms, *Does I v. Rodriguez*, alleging violations of labor standards, unjust enrichment, and human trafficking under the Trafficking Victims Protection Reauthorization Act of 2003 (TVPRA of 2003).

Difficult to Prosecute Corporations

Congress first made human trafficking illegal in the United States when it passed the Trafficking Victims Protection Act (TVPA) in October 2000. The Act defines human trafficking as either sex trafficking, "in which a commercial sex act is induced," or labor trafficking, "the recruitment, harboring, transportation, provision, or obtaining of a person for labor services, through the use of force, fraud, or coercion for the purpose of subjection to involuntary servitude, peonage, debt bondage, or slavery." In 2003, under the reauthorization of the Act, Congress established a private right of action for victims of human trafficking into or within the United States. The Trafficking Victims Protection Reauthorization Act of 2003 enables victims to sue and collect damages from their traffickers. Thus, under TVPA, those who engage in human trafficking should be both criminally liable to the State and civilly liable to their trafficking victims.

Despite the fact that under this statute traffickers are both criminally and civilly liable, the vast majority of trafficking cases go unprosecuted in the United States. The prosecution of trafficking cases against corporations is even rarer. Reaching a corporation under the trafficking statute can be difficult or even impossible. The prosecuting attorney must prove the corporation's direct involvement in the crime. For example, in *Does*, while the victims charged the Rodriguez family with two counts of trafficking, they were only able to reach Grant Family Farms, the company that largely benefitted from their trafficking, with claims of unfair labor and unjust enrichment.

Because such a statute requires proof of an agency relationship between an employee committing the crime and a corporation, the plaintiffs in *Does* were unable to charge the corporation with trafficking. The victims trying to reach Grant Family Farms are not alone: victims trafficked by agriprocessors, hotels, and other businesses encounter similar difficulties in trying to hold corporations accountable that have removed themselves from the trafficking crimes using subcontractor schemes. Due to this difficulty, many plaintiffs hoping to file suit against corporations engaged in human trafficking continue to use civil strategies established before the passage of TVPA, such as tort claims or claims under the Fair Labor Standards Act. Meanwhile, the government continues to fail to pursue criminal cases against these corporations.

In 2004, the Department of Justice created a model statute based on TVPA for all fifty states. The model law was designed to make a cohesive statutory scheme between state and federal laws in order to "prevent gaps" in legislation. States, however, have not uniformly adopted these suggestions. Several states have actually gone a step further than the federal government and passed statutes on human trafficking that explicitly include corporate liability, a provision still absent from federal legislation. . . .

Current Human Trafficking

The desire to improve one's livelihood causes many human trafficking victims to put their lives at risk. Hoping to improve the quality of life for both themselves and their families, human trafficking victims put their trust in people who promise to transport them to the United States for employment. It is from this precarious position that many end up victimized. Corporations, such as Grant Family Farms, can benefit from this free labor by employing subcontractors who arrange for the trafficking and shield themselves from liability. To examine the full context of this issue, this Section explores: (A) the prevalence of and legislation on human trafficking; (B) corporations and human trafficking; and (C) corporate liability.

Human trafficking is a widespread criminal and civil violation, often referred to as "modern day slavery." It is a major concern both internationally and within the United States. The United States government has developed statutes and case law to battle this issue.

The United Nations defines human trafficking as "[t]he recruitment, transportation, transfer, harbouring or receipt of persons, by means of the threat or use of force or other forms of coercion . . . [in order to gain] control over another person, for the purpose of exploitation." The United States, however, eliminates the element of transportation in its definition of the crime. In TVPA, the U.S. Government divided the crime of human trafficking into two parts: forced labor and sex trafficking. . . .

Due to the covert nature of the crime, estimating the number of human trafficking victims in the United States, as well as abroad, is a very difficult task. One UN report stated that the number of victims of human trafficking has risen to "epidemic" proportions. The International Labor Organization (ILO) has estimated that there are at least 12.3 million people worldwide in forced labor, bonded labor, and commercial sexual servitude. According to another estimate, there are thirty million people currently "enslaved," which, if correct, means that there are more slaves today than at the height of the Trans-Atlantic slave trade. Congress estimates that anywhere from 14,500 to 50,000 people are trafficked into the United States every year. The human trafficking industry continues to grow each day and is now the fastest growing criminal industry in the world.

Human trafficking damages victims in a variety of ways. Traffickers frequently move victims to a new location or country and strip them of any documentation. Traffickers frequently torture, abuse, starve, and frighten victims. Often traffickers sexually torture, rape, starve, and confine those transported for sexual exploitation, and similarly mentally and physically abuse those transported for forced labor while forcing them to work in brutal conditions for long hours. Additionally, many traffickers force drugs upon their victims, either to make the victims easier to control or to numb any pain.

Because of this degrading treatment, those rescued from trafficking face many problems. . . . Some may suffer symptoms of post-traumatic stress disorder. Counseling practitioners have stated that it is important victims know they are safe from their perpetrators. Studies have found that survivors frequently have resilience and a quest for meaning that assists their healing, which can be aided by seeing the prosecution of their perpetrators.

Amendments Have Strengthened the Human Trafficking Law

Before Congress established human trafficking as a crime in TVPA victims sued and prosecuted their traffickers in circulatory manners. For example, prior to TVPA, trafficking victims pursued civil suits via the Thirteenth Amendment of the U.S. Constitution, 18 U.S.C. [Section] 1584 on involuntary servitude, the Anti-Peonage Act, the Alien Tort Claims Act, as well as a variety of labor and employment laws and tort laws related to forced labor conditions. Two cases, the Reddy case and *Chellen v. John Pickle Co.*, demonstrate the circumlocutory avenues victims had to take. When TVPA went into effect in 2000, trafficking victims could finally sue and prosecute their traffickers for human trafficking.

Many human trafficking scholars use the Reddy case as the landmark example of the complex schemes human trafficking victims had to develop in order to file civil suits. A federal court sentenced Lakireddy Bali Reddy, a landlord in Berkeley, California, to more than eight years in federal prison in 2001 for smuggling teenage girls from India for cheap labor and prostitution. In addition to his prison time, the court required Reddy to pay $2 million in restitution.

Despite the success of the criminal case, it still fell short of an overall victory. Only two of Reddy's many victims received compensation, and Reddy's thriving family real-estate business continued. Thus, in 2002, a group of young Indian women filed a class-action lawsuit seeking $100 million from the Reddy family and the Reddy family businesses.

The complaint the victims filed in the Reddy case included "implied rights of action" under the Thirteenth Amendment and Anti-Peonage Act, as well as forced labor and slavery claims under the Alien Tort Claims Act (ATCA). The Northern District Court of California dismissed the claims under both the Thirteenth Amendment and the Anti-Peonage Act. The claim under the Alien Tort Claims Act was the only one that survived the motion to dismiss. . . .

As public and political consciousness of human trafficking increased, Congress passed TVPA in 2000. The Act aimed to combat human trafficking and ensure the punishment of traffickers, expressly criminalizing human trafficking. The Act also aimed to protect victims by implementing international prevention measures and providing protective services and special visas to victims.

Despite its advancements, human rights advocates criticized TVPA for its "limited and prosecutorially-focused approach," claiming that it was too focused on punishing the perpetrators rather than assisting the victims. In recognition of this issue, Congress passed the Trafficking Victims Protection Reauthorization Act of 2003 (TVPRA of 2003). In order to increase the rights of trafficking victims, this "reauthorization" gave victims the right to bring a civil action against their perpetrators. . . .

In 2008 Congress reauthorized TVPA again. The William Wilberforce Trafficking Victims Protection Reauthorization Act of 2008 (TVPRA of 2008) authorizes the funding for the

Act for the 2008 to 2011 budgets. The Reauthorization amends the Act to address issues of child labor, forced labor, and sex tourism effectively. . . .

Under this reauthorization, even someone who does not act to further the trafficking but merely consciously benefits from its existence is liable.

Corporations Use Subcontractors to Avoid Prosecution

Similar to estimating the number of human trafficking victims, determining the number of corporations involved in human trafficking crimes is impossible. The ILO estimates that eighty percent of all forced labor abuse takes place in the private markets. Trafficked labor is a profitable criminal business, generating about thirty-two billion dollars in profits per year, half of which is made in industrialized countries. One ILO report estimates that at any point 2.4 million people are victims of trafficking, the profits from which would represent an average of $13,000 per year per forced laborer.

Industries in which the ILO has identified forced labor as a major concern include agriculture, construction, garments and textiles, hospitality and catering, mining and logging, food processing and packaging, transportation, domestic service, and the sex industry. Human trafficking in the United States has also taken the form of foreign construction-recovery workers "hired" to repair oil rigs after Hurricane Katrina. The agricultural sector and factories especially benefit from trafficked workers. These industries have some of the highest demand for hard labor and thus are the most likely to turn to trafficked work.

The demand for lower prices by buyers from corporations, both within and outside of the United States, indirectly drives the number of human trafficking cases. Human trafficking is a major concern for U.S. corporations. Trafficking can be present whether corporations are conducting business abroad or not.

Corporate involvement in human trafficking within the United States usually occurs in elaborate subcontracting schemes. These schemes are similar to those employed by Grant Family Farms: a corporation hires a subcontractor to arrange for menial labor. In other schemes, the corporation may be even further removed from the crime: for example, a contractor, or coyote, convinces a victim to come into the United States, and the victim incurs a debt that he or she is told can be paid off with the promised employment. After arriving in the United States the contractor or coyote may sell the victim to a subcontractor who supplies labor to companies, similar to how a farm company sells products across the country. Since subcontractor crew leaders regulate the working conditions, growers will claim no knowledge of these conditions. Other industries, such as domestic services and factories, have similar networks. Companies can use schemes such as these to displace responsibility by turning a blind eye to the activities of its subcontractors, who frequently work outside of the United States and are seemingly unaffected by U.S. law.

Tracing the blame upwards, some non-governmental organizations have begun petitioning major food purchasers, such as Taco Bell and its parent company Yum Brands, to adopt a zero-tolerance policy for slavery and to ensure that there is no forced labor anywhere on the supply chain. Some businesses have openly aligned themselves against human trafficking by joining or pledging to campaigns encouraging accountability. For example, American Apparel and Levi-Strauss track the companies along their supply chains to ensure good labor conditions. Other companies, however, are lobbying for less accountability in supply chains. . . .

Because of the corporate structure, it is difficult for a court to hold a corporation liable for the actions of its agent. Proving the person that committed the crime is an agent of the corporation entails proving that the principal consented to the agent acting on the principal's behalf and was subject to his or her control. This can be difficult when the relationship between the principal and agent is one of buyer and subcontractor. Control consists of employers telling workers not only what to do, but also how to do it. When a subcontractor simply sells his or her services to the buyer, this element of control does not always exist.

Even if the prosecutor or plaintiff is able to prove that an individual is an agent of the corporation, the agent still must be convicted of the crime before the corporation can also be convicted. The court must impute the agent's actions . . . to the corporation; therefore, if the agent is not guilty of the crime, neither is the corporation. At times, federal courts have applied a "willful blindness" doctrine to corporations, thus sidestepping the imputing requirement. Under the "willful blindness" doctrine, the court finds the corporation criminally liable due to the corporation's conscious disregard of criminal activity. This doctrine developed through case law, but is also present in statutes. For example, the Foreign Corrupt Practices Act explicitly holds companies liable for being willfully blind to bribery and corruption of foreign officials. Application of the "willful blindness" doctrine, however, depends on the specific case, and courts have not frequently used the doctrine to impute criminal liability. . . .

Holding Corporations Liable

Under the current federal legislation, courts cannot properly hold corporations liable for their involvement in human trafficking crimes. Corporations assure their insulation from these crimes by using subcontracting schemes. Corporate civil and criminal liability would benefit both trafficking victims and society. Thus, Congress should add a provision to TVPA creating liability for corporations that are "willfully blind" to human trafficking. . . .

Human trafficking is an egregious human rights violation, occurring around the globe, including within the United

States. Because roughly thirty million people currently suffer under forced labor and sex trafficking, the perpetrators of this crime, whether they are civilians or corporations, must be brought to justice. As it stands now under federal law, corporations can only realistically be held liable for the incidents of slavery by using circulatory legislative practices. In order to improve corporate criminal and civil liability for this crime, Congress needs to pass legislation explicitly holding corporations criminally and civilly liable for "willfully blind" involvement in ventures engaged in human trafficking. This is not an impossible standard for corporations. As noted above, American Apparel and other corporations already carefully monitor their supply chains for trafficking concerns. In the latest Trafficking in Persons Report, produced as a result of TVPA, the U.S. State Department recognizes that companies need to take responsibility for the labor all the way down its supply chain. . . .

The United States enacted TVPA in order to be a global leader in the fight against human trafficking. Legislation explicitly holding corporations accountable for "willfully blind" involvement in crimes of human trafficking would represent an important step forward, both for the fight against human trafficking and the struggle to hold corporations accountable for human rights violations. Until this occurs, corporate entities will continue to benefit from the work of modern day slaves.

It Is Possible to Eradicate Modern Slavery

Kevin Bales

Kevin Bales is president of Free the Slaves and emeritus professor of sociology at Roehampton University in London. He is the author of numerous articles and books, including The Slave Next Door.

According to Bales, slavery is widespread today, and many basic commodities such as steel, produce, fish, cotton, gold, tin, diamonds, shoes, clothing, sporting goods, and rice are produced using slave labor. Despite this, antislavery efforts are underway, and Bale believes that it is possible that slavery can be eradicated. Governments need to have effective antislavery laws and to enforce them, he explains. Additionally, the work of grassroots antislavery organizations that are freeing slaves needs to be supported.

The money in Ghana has always been down on the coast. Poor religious and tribal minorities live in the North, where Ibrahim was born. Orphaned at the age of nine, Ibrahim set off with his uncle in search of work. They followed rumors to the gold mines in Ashanti state, expecting to be paid well. The jobs in the big company mines sounded perfect: training, equipment, a regular salary, and sometimes even housing were provided. Employees could even access medical care if they needed it. But when Ibrahim and his uncle reached the mining town of Obuasi, they found no jobs. Because they lacked the requisite education and recommendations, mining companies firmly turned away.

Kevin Bales, "Winning the Fight: Eradicating Slavery in the Modern Age," *Harvard International Review*, vol. 31, Spring 2009, p. 14. Reproduced by permission.

Being Trapped into Slavery

Unemployed and without any friends in the area, the two travelers became extremely hungry. Ibrahim's uncle looked everywhere for work and soon both he and his nephew fell into the hands of a gangster. He led a mining operation at a hidden deep shaft mine where gold, chiseled out by hand, was hauled to the surface one bag at a time on the backs of men and boys. Ibrahim's uncle was enlisted into an eight-person gang and advanced a little money to buy food. Too small for the hard work of hauling bags of stone, Ibrahim ran errands, fetched tools, and hauled the occasional load of rock. While his uncle kept him out of the deep mine where cave-ins were common, Ibrahim's life was no picnic. Everyone felt free to use Ibrahim as they liked, and small mistakes on his part led to beatings, sometimes with the flat side of a machete. He became the victim of the hunger and frustration that the workers felt.

After three months, the slavery trap closed. It came time for the gang organizer, a local gold buyer, to settle up with Ibrahim's uncle and the other migrant workers in the gang. The gold buyer told them that the advance of money, in addition to the other food and tools that had been provided over three months, far exceeded their share of the gold they had extracted from the mine. When the "normal" interest of 50 percent was added to the debt, it grew into what was for them a huge sum. "Don't worry," said the gold buyer, "you'll get lucky with some rich ore soon and make plenty to pay me back. Meanwhile, I'll advance you a little more so you'll have the food to keep working."

Given that they had not made enough to pay their debt, the workers even felt lucky that the gold-buyer was willing to keep them on. They felt they had no choice but agree to 50 percent interest accruing every three months. With harder work, they reasoned, they could pay off their debts easily. So they began again, working even harder and decreasing expenditures by consuming only one meal a day.

Ibrahim and his uncle had fallen into one of the most common traps that lead to slavery today. The combination of their desperation, what seems to be legitimate work, a sense of personal honor, and a snowballing debt drew them tightly under the control of a slaveholder. The trap closed fully when they learned that attempting to leave the mine would be met with violence. Under the violent control of another person, lacking freewill, being economically exploited, and paid nothing, just after his tenth birthday, Ibrahim was a slave.

Even though 2008 was the 200th anniversary year of the abolition of the slave trade in the United States, slavery is still found elsewhere and has turned up in surprising places. The trade may have been outlawed, but the practice still reaches into our homes and businesses, perhaps more than even is acknowledged. Most of us learn about modern slavery from the heart-wrenching stories of individuals like Ibrahim enslaved in the developing world, trafficked into prostitution, or forced labor in the West. But there is a larger, historic account that scholars and activists are only now uncovering as they explore the role of slavery in the global economy.

With the end of the Cold War, human trafficking and slavery have experienced a revival in business. At the same time, a global anti-slavery movement of grassroots human rights groups is emerging. National governments, regional organizations such as the Economic Community of West African States, and the United Nations have all enacted new laws and conventions to combat this epidemic. The viral nature of the innovation of slavery has necessitated the development of these new approaches. And while fighting slavery poses a challenging problem for policy makers, economists, law enforcement officials, and those who care for slavery's survivors, their efforts are encouraged by research that suggests the potential for substantially curbing this societal tragedy.

Slavery in a Modern Context

The United Nations reports that human trafficking is now the third largest moneymaker for criminals, after drugs and weapons. No one knows how many people were enslaved 50 years ago, but the number is thought to have grown rapidly since then due to the population explosion, resulting in a figure reaching an estimated 27 million today. The increase in slavery, both in our communities and in the things we buy, is also linked to economic globalization. But this is not about sweatshop workers existing on miserly wages. Slaves are under the complete violent control of another person; they are economically exploited and receive only enough food and shelter to keep them alive. For millions of victims their experiences differ little from slaves of ancient history.

The only thing truly new about modern slavery is the dramatic fall in slave prices over the past fifty years. For nearly all of recorded history slaves have been expensive, capital purchases. Over the past 3,500 years the price of slaves has averaged around US$40,000 in today's money even as the supply ebbed and flowed. But since about 1950, a glut of potential slaves has entered the market and the average price for a human life has collapsed to an all-time low of less than US$100. The supply of potential slaves is especially plentiful among the one billion people who live on about a dollar a day. In countries where high levels of official corruption mean that criminals can act with impunity, and the rule of law fails to protect the vulnerable, the poor are easily tricked or forced into slavery.

With the growth of global markets, some of these slaves are used to produce many of our basic commodities. In Brazil, for example, slaves cut down forests and burn the wood into charcoal that is then used to make steel. The United States imports over half a million tons of Brazilian steel each year to produce everything from toys to cars to office buildings. Slavery is in our fruit bowls and fridges too. There are documented cases of slaves being used to grow or harvest coffee, cocoa, sugar, beef, tomatoes, lettuce, apples, and other fruit. The list goes on: shrimp and other fish products are touched by slavery, as are cotton, gold, tin, diamonds, jewelry and bangles, tantalum (a mineral used in cell phones and laptops), shoes, sporting goods, clothing, fireworks, and rice. Recently in southern Florida, one of the largest-ever federal anti-slavery cases involved dozens of workers who picked tomatoes and oranges under guard. The produce was destined for major restaurant chains and grocery stores in the United States.

However, in contrast to the slavery of the past, while a large number of goods are tainted by modern slavery, only a very small proportion of any particular commodity has slave input. If American pre–Civil War cotton was primarily a slave-made good, the proportion of today's global cotton harvest touched by slaves may be one or two percent at most. According to a recent estimate from the International Labor Organization, the profits of human trafficking and forced labor fall in the range of US$31.6 billion. Such a figure is sizeable, but it only represents a drop in the global economic ocean.

This challenges businesses and consumers. Cocoa, for example, is grown on more than 600,000 small farms in the Ivory Coast, a country that produces about half of the good's world supply. Yet only a small fraction of those farms use slaves. Young men, normally from poor neighboring countries like Mali, come to the Ivory Coast looking for work. In remote rural areas some are tricked and enslaved by unscrupulous labor brokers and farmers. But in the West African cocoa supply chain, European and North American companies are not allowed to buy directly from the farmers. Instead, the supply filters through a series of middlemen and shippers before reaching the coast for export. The profits from slave labor are taken at the farm gate and not passed on to middlemen or processors. The global market sets the cocoa price, and farmers get the same proportion of that price whether they use slaves or not. Given the tiny fraction of farmers using slaves, their lowered labor cost doesn't pull down the market price; it just increases their profits. For that reason, boycotts of products like cocoa can actually make things worse by hurting the majority of farmers who do not use slaves.

In South Asia especially, hereditary debt bondage slavery is common. Loans are made to families suffering financial crisis (a crop failure, for example) and since the family has no other assets, they pledge themselves and all their future work as collateral until the loan is repaid. Since the moneylender now controls the family and owns all of their productive labor, it is impossible for them to accumulate assets needed to repay the debt. Trapped, the debt is passed from one generation to the next; up to 10 million people are thought to be held in what is known as hereditary collateral debt bondage slavery in India, Pakistan, and Nepal. A variant of this mechanism of enslavement ensnared Ibrahim, his uncle, and thousands of others in the illegal gold mines in Ghana.

Anti-Slavery Trends

Opposing the spread of bondage today is an emerging anti-slavery movement. This campaign confronts challenges both similar and very different to those faced at the origins of abolition in 1787. In that year, twelve men met above a printing and bookshop in London. The group planned to bring down an empire's legal slave trade, equivalent in global reach and capital to the automobile industry of today. Aligned against them were the most powerful forces of the Empire. The Church of England, for example, owned one of the largest slaveholding plantations in Barbados. That the abolitionists succeeded in their mission in a mere twenty years is almost unbelievable, especially given that their victory cost the British economy large sums extending over decades. The victory of March 1807, ending the slave trade in the Empire was the first

Workers stack sacks of cocoa in a warehouse at the port in San Pedro, Ivory Coast, in 2010. Kevin Bales uses the Ivory Coast cocoa economy as an example to illustrate the difficulty of tracing the products of slave labor. © Jane Hahn/Corbis.

of many more: the ending of legal slavery in 1833; the campaigns leadings to the abolition of slavery in the Americas by 1888; and the international Congo Antislavery Campaign at the beginning of the 20th century.

By the end of the nineteenth century, slavery was illegal in most countries with functioning legal systems. But making slavery illegal did not make it go away, just as we see today. The League of Nations and subsequently the United Nations were presented with repeated cases of slavery and human trafficking. The hereditary forms of debt bondage slavery in South Asia were relatively untouched by colonial administrations, laws passed by new national governments, or international conventions. Since 1950, factors as diverse as war, environmental destruction, corrupt governments, epidemic disease, and ethnic cleansing, all factors that disrupt the rule of law, have made populations more vulnerable to enslavement. When the end of the Cold War brought down barriers between states, the trade in people accelerated.

Since the 1980s, slavery seems to have grown more quickly than our understanding of its size and reach. But as cases of human trafficking and slavery surfaced in London, Paris, and New York, the official response was meager. In the United States this is a crime that, as a rule, goes unpunished. A strong federal law, the Trafficking Victims Protection Act, was passed in 2000. This law was exceptional in that it decriminalized victims of human trafficking, meaning that they would not be deported for illegally entering the country as well as setting high sentences for traffickers. But a significant disparity in our response is reflected in a remarkable parallel in American crime rates. If we accept the government's estimates, there are about 17,000 people trafficked into slavery in the United States in any given year; coincidentally there are also about 17,000 people murdered in the United States each year. Obviously, murder is the ultimate crime, but slavery comes a close second, especially considering the other crimes associated with it, such as rape and assault. The national success rate in solving murder cases is about 70 percent; around 11,000 murders are "cleared" each year. But according to the Attorney General's 2007 report on human trafficking, the annual percentage of trafficking and slavery cases solved is less than one percent. If 14,500 to 17,500 people were newly enslaved in America in 2006, in the same year the Department of Justice brought charges against only 111 people for human trafficking and slavery.

Industry, meanwhile, is making some progress independent of government. The Cocoa Protocol, an agreement between the European and North American chocolate industry and human rights groups and trade unions, is aimed at removing slave labor from the cocoa supply chain. The agreement, signed in May 2002, set up systems to inspect and certify cocoa at source, while mounting programs to rescue slaves and young people caught in the worst forms of child labor, as well as educating farmers. There is currently no legal requirement for companies to police their supply chain, but more than US$ 15 million has already been donated by the chocolate industry to anti-slavery projects on the ground in West Africa through an innovative joint stakeholder foundation, the International Cocoa Initiative. This model of cooperation is now being explored by other industries whose supply chains are touched by slavery.

Looking into the Future

The good news about modern slavery is that, possibly for the first time in human history, it appears that the problem can be eradicated. There exists an interesting paradox about the 27 million slaves in the world. While it may be the largest number of slaves to ever live at one point in human history, it is also the smallest fraction of the human population to ever be in slavery. Likewise, while slaves pump around US$30 billion a year into the global economy, this is the smallest fraction of the global economy ever to be represented by slave labor. With laws against it in every country, and the lack of any large vested economic interest supporting it, slavery can be ended when the public, international agencies, and governments make it a priority. Based on analysis of antislavery projects in South Asia and West Africa, the current estimated cost of the global eradication of slavery is between US$10 and US$20 billion over a 25-year period.

No single "silver bullet" policy can end slavery. Instead, a collection of policies, the investment of time, and resources will all be necessary to accomplish this worthy end. Primary among these is that national governments resource and enforce their anti-slavery laws. Brazil furnishes a very positive example of what can happen when a country takes slavery seriously. After the establishment of a Commission for the Eradication of of Slavery in Brazil, well-trained mobile anti-slavery squads began to follow up reports of enslavement. Soon the number of those freed was topping 4,000 per year. At the same time, a "dirty list" of all firms and individuals found to be using slave labor was established in Portuguese and English on the Internet. For businesses, the Cocoa Protocol represents another approach that has proven effective in removing slavery from both farms and the subsequent product chain. International development agencies can address the bondage that holds back millions of workers by applying a "slavery lens" to their work in much the same way as they successfully applied a "gender lens" in the past. These are just a few of the needed policies. They and others are needed to augment and support the immediate and crucial work of grassroots anti-slavery organizations that are bringing people to freedom every day, whether by organizing communities, fostering micro credit, or literally kicking down doors and rescuing slaves.

More good news comes from the fact that money spent on ending slavery is more an investment than a donation. Freed slaves know how to work, and they quickly begin to build assets, judging from the evaluation of anti-slavery projects. They also become what they have never been allowed to be: consumers who can buy food, clothing and education for their children. In areas with extensive slavery, liberation leads to economic growth. If we can connect the legal and economic dots, we can reasonably look to a future without slavery. Some of our strongest allies in ending slavery will be freed slaves. As more are liberated they will help guide us to better detection and better reintegration.

Human Sex Trafficking
Is Big Business

Rodney Hill and Amanda Walker-Rodriguez

Rodney Hill, a retired police lieutenant, is an assistant state's attorney in Baltimore County, Maryland. Amanda Walker-Rodriguez is also an assistant state's attorney in Baltimore County. Both are members of the Maryland Human Trafficking Task Force.

Human sex trafficking is the fastest-growing business of organized crime, Hill and Walker-Rodriguez report in the following viewpoint. When many people think of sex trafficking, they think of exotic locales in Europe, Asia, or Africa, but, the authors explain, sex trafficking also happens in cities and small towns all across the United States. Hill and Walker-Rodriguez argue that law enforcement officers at all levels must be aware of this problem and prepared to address it aggressively.

Human sex trafficking is the most common form of modern-day slavery. Estimates place the number of its domestic and international victims in the millions, mostly females and children enslaved in the commercial sex industry for little or no money. The terms human trafficking and sex slavery usually conjure up images of young girls beaten and abused in faraway places, like Eastern Europe, Asia, or Africa. Actually, human sex trafficking and sex slavery happen locally in cities and towns, both large and small, throughout the United States, right in citizens' backyards.

Appreciating the magnitude of the problem requires first understanding what the issue is and what it is not. Additionally, people must be able to identify the victim in common trafficking situations.

Rodney Hill and Amanda Walker-Rodriguez, "Human Sex Trafficking," *FBI Law Enforcement Bulletin*, vol. 80, March 2011, p. 1.

A Burgeoning Business

Many people probably remember popular movies and television shows depicting pimps as dressing flashy and driving large fancy cars. More important, the women—adults—consensually and voluntarily engaged in the business of prostitution without complaint. This characterization is extremely inaccurate, nothing more than fiction. In reality, the pimp traffics young women (and sometimes men) completely against their will by force or threat of force; this is human sex trafficking.

Not only is human sex trafficking slavery but it is big business. It is the fastest-growing business of organized crime and the third-largest criminal enterprise in the world. The majority of sex trafficking is international, with victims taken from such places as South and Southeast Asia, the former Soviet Union, Central and South America, and other less developed areas and moved to more developed ones, including Asia, the Middle East, Western Europe, and North America.

Unfortunately, however, sex trafficking also occurs domestically. The United States not only faces an influx of international victims but also has its own homegrown problem of interstate sex trafficking of minors.

Although comprehensive research to document the number of children engaged in prostitution in the United States is lacking, an estimated 293,000 American youths currently are at risk of becoming victims of commercial sexual exploitation. The majority of these victims are runaway or thrown-away youths who live on the streets and become victims of prostitution. These children generally come from homes where they have been abused or from families who have abandoned them. Often, they become involved in prostitution to support themselves financially or to get the things they feel they need or want (like drugs).

Other young people are recruited into prostitution through forced abduction, pressure from parents, or through deceptive agreements between parents and traffickers. Once these children become involved in prostitution, they often are forced to travel far from their homes and, as a result, are isolated from their friends and family. Few children in this situation can develop new relationships with peers or adults other than the person victimizing them. The lifestyle of such youths revolves around violence, forced drug use, and constant threats.

Among children and teens living on the streets in the United States, involvement in commercial sex activity is a problem of epidemic proportion. Many girls living on the street engage in formal prostitution, and some become entangled in nationwide organized crime networks where they are trafficked nationally. Criminal networks transport these children around the United States by a variety of means—cars, buses, vans, trucks, or planes—and often provide them counterfeit identification to use in the event of arrest. The average age at which girls first become victims of prostitution is 12 to 14. It is not only the girls on the streets who are affected; boys and transgender youth enter into prostitution between the ages of 11 and 13 on average.

A Highly Organized Business

Today, the business of human sex trafficking is much more organized and violent. These women and young girls are sold to traffickers, locked up in rooms or brothels for weeks or months, drugged, terrorized, and raped repeatedly. These continual abuses make it easier for the traffickers to control their victims. The captives are so afraid and intimidated that they rarely speak out against their traffickers, even when faced with an opportunity to escape.

Generally, the traffickers are very organized. Many have a hierarchy system similar to that of other criminal organizations. Traffickers who have more than one victim often have a "bottom," who sits atop the hierarchy of prostitutes. The bottom, a victim herself, has been with the trafficker the longest and has earned his trust. Bottoms collect the money from the other girls, discipline them, seduce unwitting youths into trafficking, and handle the day-to-day business for the trafficker.

Traffickers represent every social, ethnic, and racial group. Various organizational types exist in trafficking. Some perpetrators are involved with local street and motorcycle gangs, others are members of larger nationwide gangs and criminal organizations, and some have no affiliation with any one group or organization. Traffickers are not only men—women run many established rings.

Traffickers use force, drugs, emotional tactics, and financial methods to control their victims. They have an especially easy time establishing a strong bond with young girls. These perpetrators may promise marriage and a lifestyle the youths often did not have in their previous familial relationships. They claim they "love" and "need" the victim and that any sex acts are for their future together. In cases where the children have few or no positive male role models in their lives, the traffickers take advantage of this fact and, in many cases, demand that the victims refer to them as "daddy," making it tougher for the youths to break the hold the perpetrator has on them.

Sometimes, the traffickers use violence, such as gang rape and other forms of abuse, to force the youths to work for them and remain under their control. One victim, a runaway from Baltimore County, Maryland, was gang raped by a group of men associated with the trafficker, who subsequently staged a "rescue." He then demanded that she repay him by working for him as one of his prostitutes. In many cases, however, the victims simply are beaten until they submit to the trafficker's demands.

In some situations, the youths have become addicted to drugs. The traffickers simply can use their ability to supply them with drugs as a means of control.

Traffickers often take their victims' identity forms, including birth certificates, passports, and drivers' licenses. In these cases, even if youths do leave they would have no ability to support themselves and often will return to the trafficker.

These abusive methods of control impact the victims both physically and mentally. Similar to cases involving Stockholm Syndrome [in which hostages begin to sympathize with their abductors], these victims, who have been abused over an extended period of time, begin to feel an attachment to the perpetrator. This paradoxical psychological phenomenon makes it difficult for law enforcement to breach the bond of control, albeit abusive, the trafficker holds over the victim. . . .

Sex Trafficking in the USA

In December 2008, Corey Davis, the ringleader of a sex-trafficking ring that spanned at least three states, was sentenced in federal court in Bridgeport, Connecticut, on federal civil rights charges for organizing and leading the sex-trafficking operation that exploited as many as 20 females, including minors. Davis received a sentence of 293 months in prison followed by a lifetime term of supervised release. He pleaded guilty to multiple sex-trafficking charges, including recruiting a girl under the age of 18 to engage in prostitution. Davis admitted that he recruited a minor to engage in prostitution; that he was the organizer of a sex-trafficking venture; and that he used force, fraud, and coercion to compel the victim to commit commercial sex acts from which he obtained the proceeds.

According to the indictment, Davis lured victims to his operation with promises of modeling contracts and a glamorous lifestyle. He then forced them into a grueling schedule of dancing and performing at strip clubs in Connecticut, New York, and New Jersey. When the clubs closed, Davis forced the victims to walk the streets until 4 or 5 a.m. propositioning customers. The indictment also alleged that he beat many of the victims to force them to work for him and that he also used physical abuse as punishment for disobeying the stringent rules he imposed to isolate and control them.

As this and other examples show, human trafficking cases happen all over the United States. A few instances would represent just the "tip of the iceberg" in a growing criminal enterprise. Local and state criminal justice officials must understand that these cases are not isolated incidents that occur infrequently. They must remain alert for signs of trafficking in their jurisdictions and aggressively follow through on the smallest clue. Numerous Web sites openly (though they try to mask their actions) advertise for prostitution. Many of these sites involve young girls victimized by sex trafficking. Many of the pictures are altered to give the impression of older girls engaged in this activity freely and voluntarily. However, as prosecutors, the authors both have encountered numerous cases of suspected human trafficking involving underage girls.

The article "The Girls Next Door" describes a conventional midcentury home in Plainfield, New Jersey, that sat in a nice middle-class neighborhood. Unbeknownst to the neighbors, the house was part of a network of stash houses in the New York area where underage girls and young women from dozens of countries were trafficked and held captive. Acting on a tip, police raided the house in February 2002, expecting to find an underground brothel. Instead, they found four girls between the ages of 14 and 17, all Mexican nationals without documentation.

However, they were not prostitutes; they were sex slaves. These girls did not work for profit or a paycheck. They were captives to the traffickers and keepers who controlled their every move. The police found a squalid, land-based equivalent of a 19th-century slave ship. They encountered rancid, doorless bathrooms; bare, putrid mattresses; and a stash of penicillin, "morning after" pills, and an antiulcer medication that can induce abortion. The girls were pale, exhausted, and malnourished.

Human sex trafficking warning signs include, among other indicators, streetwalkers and strip clubs. However, a jurisdiction's lack of streetwalkers or strip clubs does not mean that it is immune to the problem of trafficking. Because human trafficking involves big money, if money can be made, sex slaves can be sold. Sex trafficking can happen anywhere, however unlikely a place. Investigators should be attuned to reading the signs of trafficking and looking closely for them. . . .

This form of cruel modern-day slavery occurs more often than many people might think. And, it is not just an international or a national problem—it also is a local one. It is big business, and it involves a lot of perpetrators and victims.

Agencies at all levels must remain alert to this issue and address it vigilantly. Even local officers must understand the problem and know how to recognize it in their jurisdictions. Coordinated and aggressive efforts from all law enforcement organizations can put an end to these perpetrators' operations and free the victims.

For Further Discussion

1. According to Denise Heinze and Catherine E. Lewis in Chapter 1, how do Toni Morrison's novels reflect the values of family and community instilled in Morrison by her parents?

2. An article from the *Cincinnati Enquirer* in Chapter 1 gives an account of a mother murdering her infant daughter rather than having her return to slavery. This is the real-life incident that Morrison used as the basis for *Beloved*. The article reports that some people believe the act was one of heroism, while others believe it was one of savage murder. How do you think Morrison characterizes the death of the infant?

3. In Chapter 2, Carolyn C. Denard argues that *Beloved* is not about slavery but about how the power of love enabled African Americans to maintain their humanity despite the evils of slavery. Who are some of the characters in the novel who are sustained by their love for each other and the support of the larger African American community? What actions demonstrate their humanity?

4. In Chapter 2 both Timothy L. Parrish and Jennifer L. Holden write about the impact of slavery on African American identity. Parrish writes that an African American identity was forged by slavery, while Holden writes that slavery robbed African Americans of their identity. What are the similarities and differences in the two writers' interpretations?

5. In Chapter 2 Doreatha Drummond Mbalia writes that capitalism was the cause of eighteenth- and nineteenth-century slavery, and in Chapter 3 Terrence McNally writes

that modern-day slavery is driven by profit motives. What are some of the differences that you see between slavery in the past and in the present?

For Further Reading

Maya Angelou, *I Know Why the Caged Bird Sings*. New York: Random House, 1969.

James Baldwin, *Another Country: A Novel*. New York: Dial Press, 1962.

James Baldwin, *Go Tell It on the Mountain*. New York: Dell, 1952.

Ralph Ellison, *Invisible Man*. New York: Random House, 1952.

Ernest J. Gaines, *The Autobiography of Miss Jane Pittman*. New York: Dial Press, 1971.

Zora Neale Hurston, *Their Eyes Were Watching God: A Novel*. Philadelphia: J.B. Lippincott, 1937.

James Weldon Johnson, *The Autobiography of an Ex-coloured Man*. Boston: French & Co., 1912.

Toni Morrison, *The Bluest Eye*. New York: Washington Square Press, 1970.

Toni Morrison, *Love*. New York: Knopf, 2003.

Toni Morrison, *Paradise*. New York: Knopf, 1998.

Toni Morrison, *Song of Solomon*. New York: Knopf, 1977.

Toni Morrison, *Sula*. New York: Knopf, 1973.

Toni Morrison, *Tar Baby*. New York: Knopf, 1981.

Gloria Naylor, *Mama Day*. New York: Ticknor & Fields, 1988.

Harriet Beecher Stowe, *Uncle Tom's Cabin; or, Life Among the Lowly*. Boston: J.P. Jewett, 1852.

William Styron, *The Confessions of Nat Turner*. New York: Random House, 1967.

Alice Walker, *The Color Purple.* New York: Harcourt Brace Jovanovich, 1982.

Sherley Anne Williams, *Dessa Rose: A Novel.* New York: William Morro and Co., 1986.

Richard Wright, *Native Son.* New York: Harper & Row, 1940.

Bibliography

Books

Kevin Bales, Zoe Trodd, and Alex Kent Williamson
Modern Slavery: The Secret World of 27 Million People. Oxford, UK: Oneworld, 2009.

David Batstone
Not for Sale: The Return of the Global Slave Trade—and How We Can Fight It. New York: HarperCollins, 2007.

Patrick Bryce Bjork
The Novels of Toni Morrison: The Search for Self and Place Within the Community. New York: Peter Lang, 1992.

Dillon Burroughs and Charles Powell
Not in My Town: Exposing and Ending Human Trafficking and Modern Day Slavery. Birmingham, AL: New Hope, 2011.

Elliott Butler-Evans
Race, Gender and Desire: Narrative Strategies in the Fiction of Toni Cade Bambara, Toni Morrison, and Alice Walker. Philadelphia: Temple University Press, 1989.

Karen Carmean
Toni Morrison's World of Fiction. Troy, NY: Whitson, 1993.

Jan Furman and Matthew J. Bruccoli
Toni Morrison's Fiction. Columbia: University of South Carolina Press, 1996.

Trudier Harris   *Fiction and Folklore: The Novels of Toni Morrison.* Knoxville: University of Tennessee Press, 1991.

Denise Heinze   *The Dilemma of "Double-Consciousness": Toni Morrison's Novels.* Athens: University of Georgia Press, 1993.

Jill Matus   *Toni Morrison.* Manchester: Manchester University Press, 1998.

Terry Otten   *The Crime of Innocence in the Fiction of Toni Morrison.* Columbia: University of Missouri Press, 1989.

Philip Page   *Dangerous Freedom: Fusion and Fragmentation in Toni Morrison's Novels.* Jackson: University Press of Mississippi, 1996.

Carl Plasa   *Toni Morrison: "Beloved."* Cambridge: Icon Books, 1998.

Barbara Rigney   *The Voices of Toni Morrison.* Columbus: Ohio State University Press, 1991.

Jesse Sage and Liora Kasten, eds.   *Enslaved: True Stories of Modern Day Slavery.* New York: Palgrave Macmillan, 2006.

E. Benjamin Skinner   *A Crime So Monstrous: Face-to-Face with Modern-Day Slavery.* New York: Free Press, 2008.

Periodicals

Kristin Boudreau   "Pain and the Unmaking of Self in Toni Morrison's *Beloved*," *Contemporary Literature*, Fall 1995.

Kimberly Chabot Davis   "'Postmodern Blackness': Toni Morrison's *Beloved* and the End of History," *Twentieth Century Literature*, vol. 44, no. 2, 1998.

Anita Durkin   "Object Written, Written Object: Slavery, Scarring, and Complications of Authorship in *Beloved*," *African American Review*, Fall 2007.

Cynthia S. Hamilton   "Revisions, Rememories and Exorcisms: Toni Morrison and the Slave Narrative," *Journal of American Studies*, vol. 30, no. 3, 1996.

Teresa Heffernan   "*Beloved* and the Problem of Mourning," *Studies in the Novel*, Winter 1998.

Kimberly Kotrla   "Domestic Minor Sex Trafficking in the United States," *Social Work*, April 2010.

Andrew Martin   "Slavery Becomes a Personal Question Online," *New York Times*, September 22, 2011.

John R. Miller   "Slave Trade: Combatting Human Trafficking," *Harvard International Review*, Winter 2006.

Gloria Naylor and Toni Morrison   "A Conversation," *Southern Review*, July 1985.

Barbara Schapiro   "The Bonds of Love and the
                    Boundaries of Self in Toni Morrison's
                    Beloved," *Contemporary Literature*,
                    vol. 32, no. 2, 1991.

R. Clifton Spargo   "Trauma and the Specters of
                    Enslavement in Morrison's *Beloved*,"
                    Mosaic, vol. 35, no. 1, 2002.

Donna Haisty   "Cries of Outrage: Three Novelists'
Winchell   Use of History," *Mississippi Quarterly*,
                    vol. 49, no. 4, 1996.

Cynthia Griffin   "'Margaret Garner': A Cincinnati
Wolff   Story," *Massachusetts Review*, vol. 32,
                    1991.

Internet Sources

Amy Fine Collins   "Sex Trafficking of Americans: The
                    Girls Next Door," *Vanity Fair*, May
                    24, 2011. www.vanityfair.com.

Dan Werner   "Fighting Modern-Day Slavery,"
                    Southern Poverty Law Center,
                    January 30, 2011. www.splcenter.org.

Index

A

African American community
in *Beloved*, 48–50, 64–65, 81–83, 114–115
collective experience and, 89–90
ethical code in, 47–50, 53
healing power of, 81–83
in Morrison's works, 26, 29–30
strength of, 21–23
support for Denver from, 114–115
African American culture
ethical code in, 47–50
loss of, during slavery, 76–83
in Morrison's works, 21–22, 25–27, 32–35
role of storytelling in, 9–10
values of, 20
African American families
closeness of, 23
impact of racism on, 29
separation of, under slavery, 71–72, 134
as theme, 29–31
African American history, 32–35, 44
African American identity
beauty ideal and, 24–25
internalized racism and, 103, 105–106
slavery and, 84–90, 91–102
whites and, 111
African American mothers, grief of, 81–82
African American writers, 85, 129

African Americans
female, 118–120, 126, 128–129
male, 119
solidarity of, 67–75, 89
See also Slaves
African religious beliefs, 80–81
African songs, 98–99
Alien Tort Claims Act, 150, 151
Allen, Sture, 32–35
American dream, 32–35
Angelo, Bonnie, 20, 91
Anger, 43, 79
Animal metaphors, 63, 108–109
Anti-Peonage Act, 150, 151
Antislavery movement, 158, 161–165
Assimilation, 26
Atwood, Margaret, 57, 92
Awards, 9, 25, 28, 32, 35

B

Baby Suggs (*Beloved*)
community reaction to, 48–49
death of, 129
Denver and, 102
freedom for, 121–122
home of, 109
memory of, 82
sermon by, 46–47
Sethe and, 66
on slavery, 72–73
on whites, 106, 120–123
Baker, Houston A., 63
Baldwin, James, 28
Bales, Kevin, 139, 156–165
Bambara, Toni Cade, 25

Baraka, Amiri, 22
Barr, J.L., *110*
Beauty ideal, 24–25
Beloved (*Beloved*)
    anger of, 81
    character of, 27–28, 113–115
    dance by, 98
    disappearance of, 83, 94–95,
      101–102
    ghost of, 11, 49–50, 76–78, 79,
      125
    identity of, 92–102
    lost mother of, 80, 94–95,
      100–101, 113
    as reincarnation, 11–12, 96
    Sethe and, 77–78, 97, 99–102,
      114, 132
    as Sethe's mother, 96–100
    slave ship experience of, 76–
      80, 92–99, 113–114
    smiling by, 99
    as symbol of lost cultural
      identity, 76–83
    traumatized language of, 76–
      77, 79–80, 113
Beloved (Morrison)
    awards won by, 9, 28
    film adaptation, *48*
    inspiration for, 11, 27, 36–40,
      44–45, 104
    love in, 42–53
    Middle Passage described in,
      76–80, 92–99, 101, 113–114
    mother-child relationships in,
      125–135
    plot of, 11–12, 117
    primal scene of, 92–95
    psychological trauma in, 103–
      116
    publication of, 9
    racial solidarity in, 67–75

    responses to, 42–43, 45–46,
      50–53
    slave narrative genre and,
      126–129
    slave songs in, 55–62
    slavery experience in, 27–28,
      85–90, 117–124
    themes, 9, 27–28, 30, 33–34
    white characters in, 62–64
    writing of, 27
Bhutan, 140
Bibb, Henry, 62
The Black Book (1974), 25, 26
Black community. *See* African
  American community
Black Panthers, *72*
Blacks. *See* African Americans
The Bluest Eye (Morrison), 22–25,
  28, 30, 67, 69, 112
Bodwins (*Beloved*), 72, 83, 99,
  121
Bouson, J. Brooks, 103–116
Brazil, 141, 159–160, 164–165
Brown, Claude, 22

C

Capitalism, 67–71, 74–75
Capuano, Peter J., 54–66
Carby, Hazel V., 84
Carmichael, Stokely, 22
Chain gang, 46, 61, *88*, 88–89
Chambers, Iain, 79
Child
    choice of killing, 50–52
    relationship between mother
      and, 125–135
    Sethe's killing of, 34, 44–45,
      49, 52–53, 64–65, 78, 87,
      105, 110–112, 125–126, 133–
      134

Child slavery, 141–142, 167–168
Childbearing role, of slave women, 131, 134
Christian, Barbara, 129
Cincinnati Enquirer, 36–40
Civil War, 79
Class oppression, 70–71, 74–75
Clemons, Walter, 95
Cocoa, 160–161, *162*
Cocoa Protocol, 163–164, 165
Code of ethics, 47–50, 53
Collectivism, 69–70, 74–75, 87–90
Communication, 74–75
Community
    collective experience and, 89–90
    healing power of, 81–83
    support of, 29–30
    See also African American community
Cornell University, 21, 22
Corporations, trafficking by, 146–155
Countershaming, 106
Cruelty, humor as response to, 34–35
Cultural analysis, 45
Cultural identity, loss of, 76–83

D

Darling, Marsha, 76
Davis, Angela, 25
Davis, Corey, 170–171
Debt bondage, 161, 162
Degradation, of slavery, 62–64
Denard, Carolyn C., 42–53
Denver (*Beloved*), 102, 114–116, 132
Dickinson, Emily, 30

Disremembering, 130
Douglass, Frederick, 54–64, *60*, 87, 90, 126
Drug addiction, 169

E

Economic exploitation, 70–71, 74–75, 134–135
Edwards, Thomas R., 95
Ella (*Beloved*), 49–50, 65, 82
Emasculation, 119
Emotional responses, to Beloved, 42–43, 50–53
Ethical code, 47–50, 53
Ethnography, 44

F

Family
    African American, 23, 29–31, 134
    extended, 23
    of Morrison, 18–22, 34–35
    theme of, 29–31
Faulkner, William, 22, 33, 86
Female slaves, 106–109, 118–120, 126, 128–135
Florida, 160
Forced labor, 149, 160
    See also Slavery
Forgiveness, 49, 50, 64–66, 82–83
Foster, Frances Smith, 126
Freedom, 86–87, 89, 120–123, 142–144
Freud, Sigmund, 92, 95, 97
Fugitive Slave Act, 109
Fugitive slaves, 36–40, 132

G

Gaines, Archibald K., 37–38
Garner, Margaret, 11, 27, 44–45, 104, 105
Garrison, William Lloyd, 55
Geertz, Clifford, 44
Gender oppression, 70
Ghana, 156
Ghost, of Beloved, 49–50, 76–79, 125
Ghost stories, 10
Girls, in sexual slavery, 166–172
Glover, Danny, *48*
Grant Family Farms, 147–148
Grief
     of mothers, 81–82
     over killing of child, 52
Guilt, 28, 42–43, 47, 49, 52–53
Gurang, John, 144

H

Haiti, 139–142
Halle (*Beloved*), 106–108, 118–122
Harris, Dan, 142
Harris, Trudier, 9
Heinze, Denise, 18–31
Hereditary collateral debt bondage slavery, 161, 162
Hill, Rodney, 166–172
Historical circumstances, responses to, 42–53
Historical loss, 77–83
History, 78, 80
Holden, Jennifer L., 91–102
Horvitz, Deborah, 95–96
House, Elizabeth B., 92
Howard, Richard, 92–93
Howard University, 21, 22

Hudson-Weems, Clenora, 125–135
Human spirit, 53
Human trafficking
     by corporations, 146–155
     definition, 147, 149
     harm from, 149–150
     laws against, 147–148, 150–152, 163
     prevalence of, 149, 159–160
     profits from, 160
     prosecution of, 147–148
     sex, 166–172
     in US, 145, 160, 163, 166–172
     victims of, 150
Humanity
     of characters in *Beloved*, 46–47, 56
     maintaining, 50
     of Sethe, 65
     of slaves, 54–66
     song and, 56–57, 61–62
Humor, as response to cruelty, 34–35

I

Identity
     African American, 24–25, 84–90, 103–106, 111
     of Beloved, 92–102
     collective, 88–89
     cultural, loss of, 76–83
     forged by slavery, 84–90
     personal, loss of, 91–102
     white, 111
Imperialism, 67–68
India, 140–141, 161
Individualism, 69
Infanticide
     by Margaret Garner, 44–45, 105

by Sethe, 34, 49, 52–53, 64–
65, 78, 87, 110–112, 125–
126, 133
by slave mothers, 134
Internalized racism, 103, 105–106
International Cocoa Initiative, 164
Isolation, 69, 74, 81
Ivory Coast, 160–161, *162*

J

Jazz (Morrison), 28–31, 34
Johnson, Charles, 85–90
Johnston, Harry, 92–93
Jones, Gayl, 25

K

Kastor, Elizabeth, 27
Kite, Joe, 37

L

Language
loss of, 78–81
traumatized, of Beloved, 76–
77, 79–80, 113
Latin America, 140
Leonard, John, 28
Lerner, Gerda, 119–120
Lewis, Catherine E., 18–31
Loss
historical, 77–83
of identity, 76–83, 91–102
of language, 78–81
Love
of family and community,
29–31
maternal, 81–82, 109, 112,
132, 134–135
power of, in surviving slavery,
42–53

M

Magic, 10–11
Male/female passion, 29
Malmgrem, Carl D., 11–12
Marshall, James, 36–37, 39
Maternal love, 81–82, 109, 112,
132, 134–135
Mbalia, Doreatha Drummond,
67–75
M'Baye, Babacar, 117–124
McKay, Nellie, 19
McNally, Terrence, 137–145
Memory, 78, 83, 89–90, 126, 128–
131
Middle Passage, 44, 76–80, 92–99,
101, 113–114
Milkman Dead (*Song of Solomon*),
26, 33, 104
Mine workers, 141, 157–158
Modern-day slavery
eradication of, 156–165
global problem of, 137–145
growth of, 163
sex trafficking, 166–172
statistics on, 137, 139, 163
US companies complicit in,
146–155
See also Human trafficking
Morrison, Harold, 22–23
Morrison, Harold Ford, 22
Morrison, Slade Kevin, 22
Morrison, Toni
divorce of, 22
editorial career of, 23, 25
education of, 21, 22
family of, 18–22, 34–35
life of, 18–31
marriage of, 22–23
photographs of, *24, 34*
success of, 26

teaching career of, 22
writing career of, 21–29
Mother-child relationship, 125–135
Mother(s)
of Beloved, 80, 94–95, 100–101, 113
grief of black, 81–82
loss of, 80, 94–95
of Sethe, 96–100, 118, 130
Sethe as, 81–82, 109, 131–134
slave, 130–135
Mourning, 79
Mr. Garner (*Beloved*), 72–73, 105, 121, 129, 130, 131
Mrs. Garner (*Beloved*), 129, 130, 131
Music, 20–21
Mysticism, 10

N

Nan (*Beloved*), 118
Narrative of the Life of Frederick Douglass (Douglass), 54–59, 64, 87, 126
Narrative structure, 69
Native Americans, 71
Naylor, Gloria, 77
Nepal, 140, 161
Newton, Thandie, *48*
Nkrunah, Kwame, 69
Nobel Prize, 9, 32, 35

O

Objectification, 107–109
Oppression, 28–29, 67–75, 89, 105–106, 117–124
Oral tradition, 9–10
Oxherding Tale (Johnson), 85–90

P

Pakistan, 140, *143*, 161
Paradise (Morrison), 30
Parrish, Timothy L., 84–90
Past
haunting of Sethe by, 112–113
influence of, on the present, 78, 80–83, 89–90
revision of the, 90
unspeakable, 128
Paul D (*Beloved*)
on chain gang, 46, 61, 88–89
frustration of, 73
horrors experienced by, 59–62, 71
motivation of, 46
Sethe and, 49, 101–102, 111, 115, 134–135
use of song by, 57–62, 64
Perez-Torres, Rafael, 50–60
Personal identity, loss of, during slavery, 91–102
Personhood, song and, 54–66
Phrenology, *110*
Pierce, Sarah C., 146–155
Post-traumatic stress disorder, 150
Poverty, 140
Present, influence of past on the, 78, 80–83, 89–90
Primal scene, 92–95
Princeton University, 22
Prostitution, 145, 167–168, 170–172
Pseudoscience, 107–108, *110*
Psychological trauma, 103–116
Pulitzer Prize, 9, 28

R

Racial differences, 107–108
Racial oppression, 28, 67, 68, 70–71, 105–106, 117–124
Racial solidarity, 67–75, 89
Racism
    destructiveness of, 109–112
    experienced by Morrison's family, 18–20
    impact of, 29, 103, 105–106
    racial solidarity as response to, 67–75
    scientific, 66, 107–108, 123
    slavery and, 70–71
Random House, 23, 25
Rape, 92, 118–120, 130, 145, 169
Reading, 20–21
Reddy, Lakireddy Bali, 150–151
Redemption, 142–144
Religion, African, 80–81
Rememory, 78, 79, 112, 126, 128, 130–131
Repression, 91, 97
Resistance, 112, 133–134
Richards, Beah, 48
Rodriguez, Javier, 146–147
Rodriguez, Maria, 146–147
Rodriguez, Moises, 146–147
Rothstein, Mervyn, 44
Ruas, Charles, 10
Runaway slaves, 36–40, 132

S

Samuels, Wilfred D., 125–135
Schoolteacher (*Beloved*)
    arrival of, 83
    brutality of, 59–60, 63, 112
    scientific racism of, 66, 107–108, 123
    Sethe and, 131
    Sixo and, 62
    takeover of Sweet Home by, 105, 107–109, 121–122, 130
Scientific racism, 66, 107–108, 123
Sethe (*Beloved*)
    Beloved and, 77–78, 97, 99–102, 114, 132
    community reaction to, 49, 64–65
    forgiveness of, 64–66, 82–83
    haunting of, by past, 112–113
    humanity of, 65
    infanticide by, 34, 44–45, 49, 52–53, 64–65, 78, 87, 105, 110–112, 125–126, 133–134
    memories of, 126, 129–131
    as mother, 81–82, 109, 131–134
    mother of, 96–100, 118, 130
    motivation of, 46
    Paul D and, 49, 101–102, 111, 115, 134–135
    quest for wholeness by, 129–131
    rape of, 118–120, 130
    slave experience of, 28, 105–109, 118–120, 130–131
    story of, 27
    on whites, 122–123
Sex trafficking, 149, 166–172
Sexual abuse, 71, 106–109, 118–120, 130, 169
Sexual slavery, 144–145
Shame, 104–106, 109, 111, 114–116
Shapiro, Barbara, 100
Single motherhood, 23, 81
Sixo (*Beloved*), 47, 62–64, 122
Skinner, E. Benjamin, 137–145

Slave narratives, 54–56, 58–59,
84–85, 126–129
Slave ships, 76–80, 92–99, *96*, 101,
113–114
Slave songs, 54–66
Slavery
abolition of, 126–127
African American identity
and, 84–90
brutality of, 55, 56, 59–62
child, 141–142, 167–168
as collective experience, 87–90
conditions of, 71–74
definition, 138
degradation of, 62–64
Douglass's attack on, 54–55
economic, 70–71, 134–135
effect of, on whites, 62–64
eradication of modern, 156–
165
freedom and, 86–87, 89
global problem of, 137–145
legacy of, 29, 105–106, 117–
124
loss of cultural identity from,
76–83
loss of personal identity from,
91–102
mother-child relationship and,
125–135
power of love and, 42–53
psychological trauma of, 103–
116
racial solidarity as response
to, 67–75
racism and, 70–71
repression of memory of, 91
resistance to, 112, 133–134
separation of families by, 71–
72, 134
sexual, 144–145
See also Human trafficking

Slaves
buying freedom for, 120–122,
142–144
female, 106–109, 118–120,
126, 128–135
humanity of, 54–66
objectification of, 107–109
price of, 159
runaway, 36–40, 132
storytelling by, 9
survival of, 44–46
treatment of, 71–74
Smiles, 99
Smith, Valerie, 22
Social responsibility, 69–70
Song
African, 98–99
collective identity and, 88–89
humanity and, 54–66
as key to survival, 57–59
power of, to combat despair,
59–62
slave, 54–66
Song of Solomon (Morrison), 25–
26, 30, 33, 67, 68, 69, 104
Southeast Asia, 140, 161, 162
Stamp Paid (*Beloved*), 73, 109,
115, 123–124
Stepan, Nancy, 107
Stockholm Syndrome, 170
Storytelling, 9–10, 20–21
Strouse, Jean, 19
Subcontractors, 152–154
Subjectivity, 91–92, 100–102
Sudan, 142–144
Suicide, 95, 101, 113
Sula (Morrison), 25, 28, 30, 67,
69, 112, 133
Supernatural, 10–11, 27
Sweet Home Plantation, 72–73,
105–109, 121, 126, 129–131

T

Tar Baby (Morrison), 26–27, 28, 30, 68, 69
Texas Southern University, 22
Themes, 9, 21–22, 25–31, 33–34, 42–53
Thirteenth Amendment, 150, 151
Time, cyclic nature of, 82
Totality, 30–31
Trafficking Victims Protection Act (TVPA), 146–148, 150–152, 154–155, 163
Trauma
    memory of past, 112–113
    shame and, 104–106, 109, 115–116
    of slavery, 103–116
Travis, Molly Able, 89

U

Uncanny, 97
Underground Railroad, 44, 131
United States, 145, 160, 163, 166–172
Unity, 74
    See also Racial solidarity
Universal Declaration of Human Rights, 137

V

Van DerZee, James, 28

W

Walker-Rodriguez, Amanda, 166–172

Watkins, Mel, 10
White, Deborah, 132, 133
White guilt, 42
White supremacy, 103, 104, 107–110, 123–124
Whites
    dirtiness from, 109–112
    impact of slavery on, 62–64
    oppression by, 105–106, 117–124
    sexual abuse by, 71, 106–109, 118–120
    shaming of, 106
    views on, in *Beloved*, 106, 120–123
    women, 119–120
Wholeness, search for, 129–131
Wiegman, Robyn, 104
Williams, Eric, 70–71
Williams, Lisa, 76–83
Willis, Ardelia, 18
Willis, John Solomon, 18
Winfrey, Oprah, *48*
Wofford, George, 19
Wofford, Ramah Willis, 19
Women
    black, 118–120, 126, 128–129
    sexual slavery of, 145, 166–172
    slave, 106–109, 118–120, 126, 128–135
    white, 119–120
Woolf, Virginia, 22
Wright, Richard, 26

Y

Young, Andrew, 22

3671028

CPSIA information can be obtained
at www.ICGtesting.com
Printed in the USA
FFOW05n1549310713

9 780737 763904